MATT AND TOM

ULTIMATE
FOOTBALL HEROES

RAMOS
DE GEA

FROM THE PLAYGROUND
TO THE PITCH

DINO

Published by Dino Books,
an imprint of Bonnier Books UK,
The Plaza,
535 Kings Road,
London SW10 0SZ

🐦 @dinobooks
🐦 @footieheroesbks
www.heroesfootball.com
www.bonnierbooks.co.uk

Ramos first published 2019
De Gea first published 2019
This collection published in 2020

Design and typesetting by www.envydesign.co.uk

ISBN: 978 1 78741 796 0

British Library Cataloguing-in-Publication Data:
A catalogue record for this book is available from the British Library.

Printed and bound in Great Britain by Clays Ltd, Elcograf S.p.A.
1 3 5 7 9 10 8 6 4 2

MIX
Paper from
responsible sources
FSC® C018072

ULTIMATE
FOOTBALL HEROES

Matt Oldfield delivers sports writing workshops in schools,
and is the author of *Unbelievable Football* and *Johnny Ball:
Accidental Football Genius*. Tom Oldfield is a freelance sports
writer and the author of biographies on Cristiano Ronaldo,
Arsène Wenger and Rafael Nadal.

Cover illustration by Dan Leydon.
To learn more about Dan visit danleydon.com
To purchase his artwork visit etsy.com/shop/footynews
Or just follow him on Twitter @danleydon

RAMOS

TABLE OF CONTENTS

CHAPTER 1

KING OF EUROPE

26 May 2018, NSC Olimpiyskiy Stadium, Kiev
As the referee blew the final whistle, Sergio dropped
to his knees and threw his arms in the air. Real
Madrid were once again the Kings of Europe and,
as the team captain, he was just minutes away
from lifting the Champions League trophy in front
of thousands of joyful fans. Before he could finish
that thought, he was wrapped in hugs from his
teammates.

Campeones, Campeones, Olé, Olé, Olé!

On TV screens around the world, millions of fans
watched on. 'It's another magical night to be a Real
Madrid fan,' the commentator announced excitedly.

'Zinedine Zidane continues to get the best out of this team and they have match-winners all over the pitch as we saw tonight – Cristiano Ronaldo, Gareth Bale, Karim Benzema, Luka Modrić and on and on.'

Sergio grinned as he looked around the stadium. He would be enjoying a Champions League victory lap for the fourth time, but the feeling never got old. 'Wooooo!' he said, high-fiving Luka. 'We weren't at our best, but we found a way! Now let's get the party started.'

The cameras were flocking towards Gareth, who had been the difference-maker with two second-half goals, including a spectacular bicycle kick. Meanwhile, Sergio jogged over to congratulate his manager, putting his arm round Zinedine as they waved to the thousands of Real Madrid fans in the crowd.

'Zizou, you're making life as a manager look pretty easy!' Sergio shouted, just loud enough to be heard over the cheers.

Zinedine smiled and shrugged. 'What can I say? You guys make me look good.'

It had been an emotional night for Sergio, who

had tangled with Liverpool's Mo Salah in the first half. After the Egyptian had to go off with a shoulder injury, the Liverpool fans starting booing loudly every time Sergio touched the ball.

Fouler! Cheat!

Sergio was used to making enemies on the football pitch, however. He loved the physical battles between defender and striker. There were often yellow and red cards along the way, but he almost always won the fight. And in the biggest games of all, like the Champions League Final, the Real Madrid captain was unbeatable.

As Sergio was joining in the dancing and singing with his teammates, a fan passed Sergio a Spanish flag and he wrapped it round his shoulders. They had been through some tough tests together, but that had only made their bond stronger.

'Can you believe we've won three Champions League titles in a row?' Karim called. 'No-one can say we're not the best team in the world now!'

Sergio could see the UEFA staff setting up the stage for the trophy presentation, with people

rushing around and security guards making sure
there was a safe space for the players. A man in a
smart suit was talking to some of the Real Madrid
coaches and pointing to the left-hand side of the
stage. It was trophy time!

Sergio knew the drill by now. He drifted towards
the back of the line. The captain always stood last so
he was in the right place to receive the trophy. He
waited patiently as his teammates stepped forward in
turn, shook hands and got their medals – each taking
a moment to admire the shiny design.

By the time it was finally Sergio's turn, his
teammates were already singing and jumping, arms
around each other. He grinned. It was impossible not
to. It was an incredible feeling to get the winners'
medal that they had all worked so hard for, but it
was nothing compared to being the first one of them
to get his hands on the trophy.

Once he had received his medal, Sergio turned to
his teammates. 'Ready, boys?'

They cheered and sang even louder.

Sergio reached forward and firmly gripped both

handles of the trophy. The last thing he wanted was to be seen in videos all over the Internet dropping it! He lifted the trophy, gave it one quick kiss and then raised it high above his head.

'Vamooooooooos!' he yelled.

It was one of those nights when Sergio just didn't want to leave the pitch. He could still see lots of Real Madrid fans in the crowd, savouring every moment. He clapped and waved again.

At last, it was time to take the party back to the dressing room and then to a special event at their hotel with friends and family. He couldn't wait to see his wife, Pilar, and his kids, Sergio Jr., Marco and Alejandro.

Sergio took one last look at the stadium – the confetti still scattered across the ground, the white shirts and scarves in the crowd, and the happy faces everywhere. He closed his eyes and smiled.

He still had to pinch himself at times to be sure he wasn't dreaming. The celebrations could wait an extra minute or two, he decided. He leaned against the dugout on the far side of the pitch and allowed himself to think back to his hometown of Camas where it had all begun – before the Champions League titles, before conquering the world with Spain, before signing with Real Madrid in the Galácticos era. It had been quite a journey – and it wasn't over yet.

CHAPTER 2

OLYMPIC INSPIRATION

'The game is about to start!' little Sergio called, scampering into the kitchen, before rushing back into the living room.

He jumped up onto the sofa and sat in his favourite spot – the one with the best view of the TV. It was past his bedtime, but his parents knew that there was no chance of him falling asleep anyway. School was finished for the summer and the rules had been relaxed.

'So, are you still feeling confident?' his dad, José María, asked him. 'You really think Spain can win the gold?'

The 1992 Olympic Games were being held in

Barcelona, and it was all anyone could talk about.
Sergio had been telling everyone for weeks that the
Spanish football team was destined to do well.

'Of course!' he replied. 'Our team is great – Kiko,
Pep Guardiola, Luis Enrique… *and* we're playing at
home. You just wait and see!'

'Sergio knows his stuff,' his mum, Paqui, added.
'Who knows – maybe one day that'll be you out
there playing for Spain!'

Sergio loved that idea, but for now, he was ready
to cheer on his national heroes in their opening
match against Colombia. Within minutes, he was
running through the living room as Guardiola put
Spain ahead.

*Goooooooooooooooooooooaaaaaaaaaaaaaaaallllllllllll
llllllllllllll!!!!!!!!!!!!!!!!!!!!!!!*

By now, René, his older brother, had joined the
party. They high-fived and sat side-by-side on the
sofa. His sister, Miriam, perched on the armrest.

Spain were already ahead of Colombia by 3–0 at
half-time and Sergio could just sit back and enjoy
the game. He loved how the Spanish players passed

the ball so effortlessly around the pitch, waiting for the right moment to pounce. They were off to the perfect start.

That night, Sergio lay on his bed holding his favourite football, which was scuffed and slightly ripped from many hours of use. He threw it into the air and caught it again. How was he meant to sleep after watching that game? He wanted to be outside, pretending that he played for Spain!

The next afternoon, he dribbled that same ball to the park with his friends, Felix and Fernando. Like him, all they wanted to talk about was Spain's chances of winning the gold medal. They set up a goal with two jumpers and took turns pretending to be Luis Enrique.

'Cross it in!' Sergio called out as Felix dribbled forward. Every time one of them scored, they recreated the goal celebrations they had watched the night before.

By the end of the group stage, Sergio's prediction was starting to look good. Spain finished top of their group, then sneaked through to the semi-finals.

Sergio had been biting his nails throughout the quarter-final, but Paqui decided it was not the time to make a comment to her son.

As Spain kept winning, Sergio was more and more glued to the action. José María could only smile – his youngest child had shown a flicker of interest in football before that summer, but now it was all he thought about.

'We can't miss the game,' Sergio pleaded on the day of the semi-final against Ghana as the family left the house for a picnic. 'I'm their lucky charm!'

'Don't worry,' José María said, laughing. 'We'll be back in plenty of time for you to change into your lucky shirt, get a drink in your lucky cup and sit at your lucky end of the sofa.'

Sergio smiled. 'Sorry, just checking.'

The Ramos house had a Spanish flag in the window along with all the different red and yellow decorations that were being given out all over the country for the Olympics. As promised, they were all back from their picnic well before kick-off and Sergio had time to watch all the pre-game build-up.

He joined in with the national anthem and then silence fell over the whole house as the game began. Even through the TV, Sergio could hear the crowd roaring for Spain to make a good start – and they did, with Abelardo, a defender, scoring.

'Yes!' Sergio clapped his hands and jumped up off the sofa.

'See, Sergio, defenders can still score goals,' José María teased. He often tried to tell his son that it wasn't always the strikers who got the glory.

Spain scored a second goal after half-time, moving a step closer to the Gold Medal Game. René stood up. 'Game over,' he said.

In a flash, Sergio picked up a cushion and threw it in his brother's direction. 'Don't say that!' he shouted. 'You'll jinx us. There's still time for Ghana to come back. We have to stay focused.'

'When did you start managing the team, little bro?' René shot back, laughing. 'You're right, though. If Ghana score now, it'll be a nervy finish.'

'Well, it'll be your fault if they do!' Sergio said, with a look that said he was only half-joking. But

there was no reason to worry. Spain held on for a
2–0 win, setting up an even bigger game against
Poland in the final just three days later.

But that felt like a long wait for Sergio. When
the Gold Medal Game finally arrived, he was too
distracted to eat his breakfast.

'My stomach is doing backflips,' he explained,
lying on the sofa. 'Just give me a minute.'

'Kiko and Luis Enrique are probably nervous too,'
Paqui said. 'But they have to eat, otherwise they'll
have no energy for the match.'

'Good point,' he said, slowly sitting up and joining
the family at the table.

By kick-off, Sergio was already pacing around
the living room. 'Win or lose, we should all be very
proud of the team,' Paqui explained, fearing how
Sergio would react if Spain lost.

But Sergio barely heard her. He was too busy
watching the Spain players walking down the tunnel
and onto the pitch. Their red shirts looked even
cooler today.

Over the next two hours, Sergio went through

every possible emotion. He had his head in his hands when Poland scored first, then there was relief and joy as Spain came back to lead 2–1. Then frustration as Poland made it 2–2 almost immediately. Now, extra time was looming.

With ninety minutes on the clock, Spain won a corner. 'Come on, one last chance,' Paqui said, with her hands over her face. Sergio was silent, just praying for a late winner.

The ball came in and was cleared to the edge of the box.

'Shoot!' the family all shouted.

The ball was blocked but it rebounded straight to Kiko.

'Yes! Yes!' Sergio screamed.

The keeper was already on the floor, having dived for the first shot. Kiko took a quick touch and calmly lifted the ball into the net.

'Gooooooooal! We've won it! We've won it!' Sergio yelled, running to hug everyone.

'Wow!' José María, René and Sergio's sister Miriam all said at once.

They cheered even louder when they saw the replay of the goal.

The phone rang. It was one of José María's friends. He rushed out of the room and was back within a minute. 'That was Jorge. He's going to drive around Camas to see the celebrations. Do you mind if I go?'

'No problem – go for it,' said Paqui. 'But take the kids. They'll love it!'

Sergio raced to the front door, put on his shoes in record time, and then followed José María, Miriam and René out to the car. They drove around Camas, honking the horn all the way and singing songs with friends and neighbours.

España! España! España!

'What a night!' Sergio shouted, hugging René. In his head, he was imagining himself playing football for Spain one day. 'It must be amazing to give the fans a moment like this!'

CHAPTER 3

PEPITO THE SECRET WEAPON

The Olympics had put Sergio firmly on the football path. That continued as he played more often at the park, often begging René to let him join in with the older kids when they needed an extra player, or tag along for his Camas Juniors practices.

'Please can I play? Pleeeeaaaase – I won't let you down, I promise!'

One morning, he finally got his wish. Paqui hurried down the stairs and packed shorts and socks into René's bag.

'Change of plans,' she called, stopping to catch her breath. 'Sergio, you're coming with us to René's practice and then we'll go straight to the festival.'

Sergio grinned and rushed to the front door quickly before his mum could change her mind. He loved watching his brother play, and he would get to dribble his ball around and take some practice shots on the pitch opposite.

René looked over at his younger brother as they left the house. 'I don't mind you coming to the practice, but just don't say anything embarrassing in front of my friends.'

They weaved their way through the narrow streets of Camas and turned into the car park just in time. Sergio saw the familiar faces of René's teammates on the nearest pitch starting their warm-up.

'Okay, out you get,' Paqui said.

René undid his seat belt and hopped out to join his friends. Paqui turned to Sergio as he followed his brother. 'Sergio, remember, just stay close. I'll be here if you need me.'

Sergio nodded and dribbled over to the touchline to get a closer look at the action. He could see René's coach laying out cones and pointing for the boys to line up on the edge of the penalty area.

As Sergio flicked the ball up and trapped it expertly with his right foot, he felt a hand on his shoulder. He turned to see Nando, one of René's best friends.

'Hey, Sergio,' he said. 'So, is this some kind of punishment? Watching your brother play football can be tough on the eyes.'

Sergio laughed. 'I'll tell him you said that!'

'Please do! Are you getting to play much yet?'

'Just with friends at the park. Hopefully my parents will sign me up for a proper team next season.'

'Cool! Come and take some shots. I'll go in goal.'

Sergio paused. 'Wait, why aren't you training with the others?'

'I hurt my knee last week and they want me to rest it. Don't worry – I won't be diving around.'

'Okay, you're on!'

Sergio suddenly felt a bit nervous as he walked over. He knew Nando was a good player and he didn't want to make a fool of himself.

He lined up the ball near the penalty spot, took a few steps backwards and kicked it as hard as he could. His shot went straight at Nando, who saved it easily, but Sergio was pleased with the power.

'Nice one!' Nando called out. 'Just angle your foot a bit to aim it into the corner.'

Sergio had another try, going for the same power but better direction. He looked up to see the ball sweeping into the bottom corner.

Goooooooooooooooooooooaaaaaaaaaaaaaaaaaallllllllllll llllllllllllllllll!!!!!!!!!!!!!!!!!!!!!

He tried to hide his excitement, but a smile quickly spread across his face.

'Perfect!' Nando shouted as he picked the ball out of the net. 'You'll be teaching your brother how to play in no time!'

Sergio felt ten feet tall. Now he had the confidence to run back to the halfway line and dribble forward for his next shot – a little touch with his right foot, right foot again, then left, then right. As he got into the penalty area, he took one quick look at the goal and poked the ball into the net.

Goooooooooooooooooooooaaaaaaaaaaaaaaaaaallllllllllll llllllllllllllllll!!!!!!!!!!!!!!!!!!!!!

Sergio had forgotten all about René's practice. He loved that he had the chance to test himself.

After a few more shots, Nando walked over and patted Sergio on the back. 'You've got a lot better since I last saw you. Keep it up.' He handed the ball back to Sergio. 'I better go before I get in trouble with the coaches.'

Sergio went back over to watch his brother.

By now, they had split into teams of three to play matches on small pitches. He could hear one of the coaches shouting instructions, reminding the boys to focus on one-touch passes.

As he waited for the practice to finish, he dribbled up and down the touchline – first at a slow, careful pace and then faster and faster. He was sweating now and stopped near the corner flag to catch his breath.

He looked up to see one of the coaches walking over. His heart sank. Was the coach angry that Nando had been risking his knee injury to play with him? His mind spun round quickly as he tried to think of what he would say.

But as the coach got closer, Sergio could see that he was smiling. Maybe this was about something else.

'You're René's brother, right?'

Sergio nodded.

'I'm Hector, one of the main coaches working with Camas Juniors. Do you want to join in with us? We could use another player to even up the teams.'

Sergio's mouth dropped open. 'Yes, sure,' he finally managed to reply, then immediately wondered what René would say.

He followed Hector over to the pitch and retied his shoelaces.

Lolo, the other coach, was now sorting the boys into two teams to play on a bigger pitch. 'Lolo, we've got one more here,' Hector called, pointing to Sergio.

René laughed, putting an arm round Sergio. 'I should have known there was no chance of you just kicking the ball around quietly!'

Once the game started, Sergio loved every minute of it. He couldn't kick the ball as hard or as far as the other boys, but he raced around the pitch and made a couple of clearances.

Then the ball deflected towards him. He controlled it well, looked up and poked a quick pass to René, who drilled a low shot into the bottom corner.

'Great pass, little bro!' René said, putting Sergio in a playful headlock.

As the boys scooped up their water bottles at the end of the practice, Lolo joined René and Sergio.

'Well done today – both of you. Sergio, you've got great instincts and you don't even seem tired after all that running. Are you already signed up for a team this year?'

Sergio shook his head, and a little smile appeared in the corner of Lolo's mouth.

'How would you like to sign with Camas Juniors?'

Sergio was stunned and confused.

René had the same look of shock on his face. 'I like playing with Sergio, especially when he gives me passes like that one today, but he's only seven. Isn't our league really strict on checking ages? If he's not nine yet, how can he play?'

But Sergio could see from Lolo's face that he had a plan. 'Well, we might be in luck here. We've got a

completed registration form for a boy called Pepito,
but his dad had to change jobs, so they've moved to
another town. I'm thinking you could play as Pepito.
What do you think?'

At first, Sergio and René both laughed, but then
they realised that Lolo was serious. 'Really?' Sergio
asked.

'I don't usually like to bend the rules, but a player
with your energy would really help us and the season
is only a few weeks away.'

'Wow, okay. I'll have to ask my mum and dad,
but I'm sure they'll let me play. They've got to drive
René to games anyway.'

René nodded. 'Welcome to the team, Pepito!'

They all burst out laughing.

CHAPTER 4

DREAMING BIG

Señor Nunez waved his hands and whistled to get his class's attention. 'This morning, we're going to get into groups to talk about the types of jobs you might like to do when you're older. That might seem like a long way away – and it is – but it's a good exercise to get you thinking.'

He took a piece of chalk and started writing on the board, giving the class some examples to consider.

'Some of you might like to teach, like me.' He paused and grinned at the silence in the room. 'I guess not! Maybe a doctor or a racing car driver is more exciting. See what you can come up with.'

He split the class into five groups and then

walked around the room listening to the different conversations.

'I used to think I wanted to be a matador and put on a show for a big crowd,' Sergio explained to his group, as Señor Nunez appeared and sat on the edge of the desk. 'But now that I've started playing football every week, I've changed my mind. I'm going to be a professional footballer in La Liga!'

His teacher looked at him with a raised eyebrow. 'Sergio, having a dream to chase is never a bad thing, but you also have to remember that only the very best can play football as their job. It's important to have other options too.'

'But football is all I want to do,' Sergio insisted. 'I love it. If I work hard enough, I know I can do it.'

Señor Nunez nodded. 'Well, you've certainly got the right attitude. Just keep an open mind about a Plan B.'

He didn't want to upset Sergio, but he felt a responsibility to be honest about the difficult odds of becoming a footballer. He had seen it before – so many good young players were fighting to get into

the big academies and there were no guarantees. But
Sergio was clearly talented. Señor Nunez had heard
the stories about lunchtime hat-tricks and weekend
victories. Maybe he could beat the odds, after all.

When Sergio got home from school, he went
straight to the back garden and started knocking
a ball back and forth against the wall, testing his
reactions as it pinged back towards him. Then he
switched to keepy-ups. He was determined to prove
his teacher wrong.

Hearing the sound, Paqui looked out of the
kitchen window. She knew the signs with Sergio.
Something had made him angry.

'What's wrong, Sergio?' she called. When he
didn't reply, she walked outside and asked him
again.

Sergio picked up the ball. Sweat was pouring
down his face. 'Nothing really. Señor Nunez told
me that it's really hard to become a professional
footballer, but I'm going to show him I can be that
one out of thousands who makes it.'

Paqui smiled. She had learned long ago not to

make the kind of mistake that Sergio's teacher had made. When her son set his heart on achieving something, he was an unstoppable force.

'Just be careful, darling,' she pleaded. 'You're already playing against older kids at the weekend. I don't want you to be too tired or fall behind at school.'

'I've got it covered,' Sergio replied with a wink. 'You worry too much, Mum!'

The back garden practices became a regular event as he tried to improve his ball control, passing and shooting. Sometimes René joined in, and José María too. Sergio put sticks in the ground to dribble in and out of when he was by himself, and two tall, skinny trees were the perfect goalposts. Often, he was out there until the last sliver of sunlight had gone.

René was still bigger and stronger than his younger brother, but Sergio made up for it with his energy and fearlessness. Plus, he was getting more and more skilful. One night, just after Paqui had given them the five-minute warning for dinner, Sergio wrong-footed René with a quick change of direction and smashed a low shot into the imaginary bottom corner, glancing off the inside of the tree trunk.

José María and René exchanged a quick glance that silently said: 'Wow, Sergio is getting really good!'

Sergio pretended not to see it, but he could hardly contain a grin as he jogged back down the garden.

CHAPTER 5

SCOUTED BY SEVILLA

Sergio started off as a secret with Camas Juniors, but it did not stay that way for long. The more he played, the faster his game developed, and he was soon one of the first names on the team sheet.

Then one Saturday, when he was ten years old, his world was turned upside down. For weeks, he had heard stories from friends about scouts coming to watch local games. Each time, he had laughed at the idea, but deep down that extra pressure made him nervous. What if he made a bad mistake? Would the scouts know that he was younger than the rest of the boys?

'Try not to think about that,' José María said,

sensing that Sergio was getting distracted. 'It's just another game. Go out and enjoy yourself.'

Lolo had a similar message for the team. 'Don't try to be the hero and do too much on your own. Play as a team – the way we always do.'

Sergio felt sharp. It was usually at the end of games that his energy stood out, as other boys got tired. But today he felt a step quicker than everyone else, right from the first whistle.

One minute he was sprinting towards a loose ball and playing a quick pass down the line, the next he was winning two tackles to stop a counter-attack. Sergio knew he was rarely the most skilful player on the pitch, but he made up for it with his speed and his brain.

At half-time, José María put an arm round Sergio. 'Awesome!' he said quietly. 'That's the best half I've ever seen you play.'

At the end of the game, Sergio was exhausted. He limped over with his teammates and sat down on the grass, breathing heavily. Usually his dad came over with Sergio's water bottle and some words of encouragement – but not today. He spotted José María on the opposite side of the pitch and saw his dad talking with a tall man in a tracksuit. Sergio had never seen him before.

'Well done today,' Lolo was explaining, but Sergio was only half-listening. Who was this mystery man talking to his dad?

Finally, his dad appeared and weaved his way through the tired boys gathered around their coach. He ruffled Sergio's hair and passed him his water. Sergio turned to thank him and saw a huge smile on his dad's face. José María winked and then walked away, not wanting to interrupt the coach's post-game talk.

When it was time to go, Sergio rushed over to his dad, ready to ask a hundred questions. José María had been planning to keep it a secret until they were back in the car, but when he saw the excited look on his son's face, the words just tumbled out.

'You're not going to believe this, Sergio,' he began. 'A scout from Sevilla was at the game today and you really impressed him! He wants you to come for some training sessions at their academy. The director is going to phone tonight with more details.'

Sergio's legs turned to jelly. 'Wow!' was all he managed to say. He had hoped that the mystery man might be a scout, but he hadn't dared to dream.

That night, José María, Paqui and Sergio waited patiently for the call from Sevilla. Just before nine o'clock, the phone rang, and his dad hurried to the kitchen to answer it.

'Hello, José María speaking.'

'Hi there – sorry to call so late. This is Pablo Blanco, director of the Sevilla academy. I got a glowing report from one of my scouts today about Sergio – he's clearly a natural. You must be very proud.'

'Thank you – we are. Sergio just loves to play football.'

'Well, there's obviously potential there. We'd like to offer Sergio an eight-week trial at the academy, starting on Wednesday. Training starts at seven o'clock, but can you come in a little earlier to sign the paperwork? Then we'll introduce Sergio to the coaches.'

As Pablo was talking, José María took a second to give Sergio a thumbs-up. 'That's fantastic,' he replied. 'Yes, we'll be there!' René and Miriam had heard the phone ring and appeared in the doorway.

When José María put the phone down, he turned to the rest of his family.

'Wrong number, I guess,' he said, laughing.

'Yeah, right,' Sergio replied, grinning. 'Come on, what did they say?'

'Do you have any plans on Wednesday night? If not, you'll be training with the Sevilla academy. They're giving you a trial!'

'Wooooooooooooo!' Sergio, René and Miriam shouted all at once. They came together with their parents for a big family hug.

'Congratulations, little bro,' René said. 'This could be the start of something really special. Just remember that I'm the one who taught you everything you know!'

'I've got to call my friends and tell them the

news,' Sergio said suddenly. 'What a day! They won't believe it!'

But José María was already holding up one hand to put an end to that plan. 'It's late, Sergio. They'll be in bed. That's where you need to be too.'

He expected big protests from Sergio about how he would never be able to sleep with all the excitement, but his son just nodded. 'You're right. I can't be tired on Wednesday.' He disappeared and came back in his pyjamas to say goodnight.

The next three days were painfully slow for Sergio. One minute, he was nervous about whether he would be good enough to compete against boys who had probably been at the academy for a few years already. The next minute, it was pure excitement. His friends talked about it non-stop, and asked a barrage of questions. Would he meet the players? Would he be practising at the stadium? What would he be doing in the sessions?

Sergio had none of the answers, though. 'You'll have to wait for Thursday morning,' he said. 'No bad tackles in the playground until then, please.'

On the Wednesday afternoon, both Sergio and his father hurried home.

'We can't be late, Sergio,' José María called. 'There's some chicken and rice in the fridge. Start eating that and then get changed.'

The car journey to meet with Pablo was mostly a quiet one. Sergio looked out of the window and thought about what he would say when he met the other boys.

'You're going to be great,' his dad said, mainly to break the silence and help Sergio relax. 'But the most important thing is to have fun. If you do that, good things will happen.'

A smiling man met them at reception and then Pablo appeared from one of the hallways. 'José María – nice to meet you! And this must be Sergio. Welcome to the Sevilla academy. Follow me.'

They made their way to a big office with windows that looked out onto the pitches below.

'Okay, we'll get to the forms and signatures in a minute. That part is easy. But first, Sergio, I want you to know that we're very excited to have you here with us at Sevilla. I'm sure you'll get on very well with the other boys and all the coaches.'

There was a knock on the door. 'Ah, perfect timing. José María, we can finish the paperwork together. Sergio, there are some people I want you to meet. Come in!'

A man in a tracksuit with a friendly face walked in.

'This is Agustín, who will be coaching you tonight,' Pablo explained. 'He runs the Under 10s team.'

Sergio stood up and shook hands. He wasn't sure how much to say, so he settled on 'I can't wait to get started.'

Two boys appeared behind Agustín, who promptly introduced them. 'Sergio, this is Antonio and this is Javier. We wanted there to be a few familiar faces by the time you get out onto the pitch.'

Sergio shook hands again.

'Boys, can you show Sergio around? There's a training top for him in the changing room. I'll see you out on the pitch in twenty minutes.'

Sergio said bye to Agustín, Pablo and his dad, then followed Antonio and Javier.

'The coaches make everything really fun,' Antonio said. 'I'm sure you'll enjoy it.'

'I remember being pretty nervous at my first training session, but it went away as soon as they got the balls out and we started playing,' Javier added, and then he came to a stop. 'Here we are – this is where we get ready.'

Javier was right. It didn't take long for Sergio to shake off the nerves. During the warm-up, he hit a couple of crisp passes and managed to match the others' pace on their laps of the pitch. From then on, he felt at home.

Even so, Sergio still needed to give the Sevilla youth coaches a reason to keep him around. When they switched to five-a-side games, Sergio sensed his chance to shine. He was everywhere, sprinting back to make important tackles, playing the simple pass and even scoring a couple of goals. When Agustín called for a water break, Sergio bent over, panting, and tried to catch his breath. His legs ached, he had a cut on his knee that was bleeding, and his shirt was soaked with sweat. But he was loving it.

At the end of the practice, Agustín gathered the boys together. 'Great session today,' he said. 'You moved the ball well and we were sharp around the box. Sergio, you looked right at home with us too. Great job.'

Sergio felt a shiver of excitement and tried to play it cool as some of the other boys looked over at him. Even after showering and changing, he still had a big smile on his face. When he saw his dad waiting for him outside, he noticed that he was grinning too.

'So, how was the first practice?' José María asked.

'Amazing!' Sergio said. 'At first, I was nervous, but I was just as good as the other boys, and you should have seen one of my sliding tackles!'

José María laughed. 'Only you would dish out some bruises in your first academy session!'

'I can't wait for the next practice! I just hope I can do enough to make them keep me for longer.'

'It's funny you should say that,' José María

replied. 'Agustín came to see me while you were getting changed. He's already talking about signing you!'

Sergio's mouth dropped open, but no words came out. He just smiled all the way home.

CHAPTER 6

ANTONIO AND JESÚS

Sergio was one of the fastest rising stars in the
Sevilla academy, but his progress was not without
challenges. For a start, he could play in a few
different positions and that meant he got moved all
over the pitch. He also spent some time watching
from the touchline after injuring his leg. But through
it all, he had first Antonio Puerta, then Jesús Navas
too, to turn to. Whatever the situation, the 'three
amigos', as they liked to call themselves, were there
for each other.

Antonio liked to think of himself as the wise old
man. He had been at the Sevilla academy the longest
and knew everyone around the place, from the

cafeteria ladies to the cleaners. He and Sergio moved
through the Under-11s, Under-12s and Under-13s
together, sweeping aside every team they faced. With
Sergio now fit again after missing their Under-14
season, he was ready to face the best Under-15
teams in the country – and now they had Jesús, the
new kid on the block, on the team too. Antonio and
Sergio liked him from the very first practice.

Sergio was spending more and more time at the
academy, training a few times a week, and then
coming in to put in extra work between sessions.
More often than not, at least one of the other amigos
was with him.

Their friendships made a big difference on the
pitch. Since all three were playing in midfield, they
knew exactly where each other would be at all
times. Whether it was a perfect through ball or a
pinpoint cross, they had an unspoken understanding
of how to play football.

During one away game, Sevilla were losing 1–0,
before the three amigos turned it around. 'We're not
losing this,' Sergio said to Antonio and Jesús as the

second half began. First, Sergio beat two defenders and squared the ball to Jesús for a tap-in. Then Antonio skipped through, rounded the keeper and was tripped up. Before the referee could blow the whistle for a penalty, Sergio had pounced on the loose ball and fired it into the net.

'The three of us are unstoppable,' Antonio said as they sat outside at the Ramos house eating ice cream. He had become a regular visitor there and both Paqui and José María thought he was a great influence on Sergio. He went on: 'Sometimes I think about what it would be like if we all got into the first team together.'

'We'd have so much fun,' Sergio added. 'The coaches would never be able to get us to stop talking, but they'd still love us!'

'Plus, we'd get to hang out even more. That means more card games, more films, more parties.'

'Life doesn't get much better than that,' Jesús said.

They all laughed. They were living the dream.

'Most of all, it's pretty cool to get to play the game you love with great friends,' Sergio said. 'The academy would be a lonely place in some ways if we hadn't met.'

Their run of wins continued – one week 4–0, the next week 5–1. At school, word spread about their success with Sevilla, but all that attention didn't change them. René was always the first to bring Sergio back down to earth if he got too cocky. 'It's for your own good, little bro,' he liked to say, wagging his finger. 'You'll thank me one day!'

But that kind of advice was rarely needed. The three amigos were usually too busy talking about the last game, thinking about the next one and planning their eventual domination of La Liga as Sevilla's biggest stars.

CHAPTER 7

ON THE FAST TRACK TO THE TOP!

Sergio pinged the ball across to Jesús, who controlled it on his chest and passed it back.

'I'm telling you, Jesús, we're going to win the Under-16 League and the Cup this year,' Sergio said. 'I've got a good feeling about it.'

Jesús grinned. 'You always say that about everything! Seriously, when was the last time you had a bad feeling about anything?! But this time you might be right.'

'We're going to surprise people. With you on one wing, Antonio on the other and me at the back, we can beat anyone.'

Sergio was playing more and more in defence,

using his speed to cut out through balls and his passing to start attacks. He had grown too and was winning lots of headers.

Toni, one of the newer coaches, called the players together and they set off on a few laps around the pitch.

At the end of training, Sergio felt a tap on his shoulder. 'Just hold on a minute,' Toni said, looking around to check whether the other players had all started walking back inside. 'Another good session today. Well done.'

'Thanks, Coach.'

'You'll thank me even more when you hear this.'

Sergio looked up, confused but excited.

'I got a call this morning from Joaquín Caparrós. He's been keeping a close eye on you.'

The first team boss! Sergio grinned. He had seen the first team coaches at practices and games occasionally, but they had usually gone by the time the sessions finished.

'I'll get right to the point. Caparrós wants you to start training with the first team.'

Sergio tried to look calm but inside he was jumping up and down. He was going to be sharing the same pitch with the players he watched on TV every weekend.

When he got dropped off at home, Sergio raced up the street and bundled through the door. 'Mum! Dad!'

His parents rushed out of the kitchen, with panic on their faces. 'What's wrong?' Paqui asked.

'Nothing – sorry, I didn't mean to scare you. I just have big news and I couldn't wait to tell you.'

'What? Tell us!'

'I'm going to be training with the first team!'

They rushed over and wrapped Sergio in a big hug.

'My son is going to be training with the Sevilla first team!' José María kept saying over and over.

Once Sergio had finished telling all his friends and family, the excitement was at least partly replaced by nerves. What if it was a big disaster? He was only sixteen and now he would be playing against men.

Just then, his phone rang. It was Jesús.

'Congrats, mate. I just saw your text.'

'What if I blow this chance, Jesús? I've worked so hard over the last few years. We all have.'

'You won't. I know you and so do the coaches.

They wouldn't have called you up if they didn't think you were ready to take this next step. I bet they'll all give you a warm welcome. If you play like you always do in our practices, you'll be fine.'

'Thanks. I've just got a lot on my mind and this is all happening really fast.'

'That's what I'm here for. We'll miss you, though. I guess that's the end of our plan to win the league and cup together.'

'No,' Sergio replied instantly. 'It means that we're going to do it together in the first team. Just wait and see.'

The next day, he got dropped off at the training ground extra early. He couldn't risk being late on his first morning with the first team.

Caparrós spotted him roaming the corridors and called him over.

'Couldn't sleep?' he asked, smiling.

Sergio blushed. 'Something like that,' he replied.

'This is a big moment for me.'

'It is,' Caparrós agreed. 'But try not to over-think it. We believe in you and you're going to get plenty of chances to learn. The lads are excited to meet you.'

Caparrós introduced him to a few of the players, and then – once they were out on the pitch – gave him a proper welcome in front of the whole squad.

The first session went well. His control was good, and he felt confident enough to use both feet, even though he was always more comfortable on his right foot. If anything, he got a bit *too* confident. During one of the exercises, he was one of the two 'piggies in the middle', closing down other players as they tried to knock the ball around the circle. As he sprinted around, he spotted a pass that was hit a little too softly. In a flash, he lunged forward and poked the ball away, but at the same time he collided with one of his teammates.

Sergio turned to see that he had injured Pablo Alfaro, the Sevilla captain and one of the toughest, most feared defenders in La Liga. His heart skipped a beat – this was the last person he wanted as an enemy. He walked over slowly and put his hand on Pablo's back. 'Sorry. I didn't see you.'

Pablo gave him a long stare, and then broke out into a little grin. 'No worries, kid. That was a tackle I'd be proud of.'

Sergio was thrilled to be learning so much from his older teammates – and his coaches seemed to be really pleased with his progress. One January afternoon, Caparrós walked over to the pitch with Sergio and, without any big build up, said:

'You'll be on the bench on Wednesday night against Deportivo. We're really impressed with the way you've trained over the past few weeks and now it's time to start getting you some playing time.'

'This isn't a joke, is it?' Sergio answered, laughing. He was still only seventeen years old. 'Don't do that to me!'

Caparrós smiled. 'That would be so cruel! No, I'm serious.'

As he climbed the steps onto the team bus for the

drive to the airport, Sergio had butterflies. He was travelling with all the same players that he trained with every day, but somehow this felt different. He was making his La Liga debut!

With Sevilla losing 1–0 to Deportivo, Sergio started warming up again, stretching and jogging up and down the touchline. On his way back to the dugout, Caparrós signalled for him to come over.

'We're sending you on in five minutes for Francisco so stay ready.'

'Will do, boss.' Sergio hoped his voice didn't sound too nervous. His heart was racing.

He finished a few more stretches and started taking off his tracksuit. He wondered if his friends and family at home could see him. He was sure there would be a lot of calls and texts flying around.

The ball was cleared out for a throw-in and the referee stopped play for the substitution. Sergio was coming on! He jumped up and down a couple of times, high-fived Francisco and then ran on to join his teammates.

With less than thirty minutes of the game left,

Sergio – playing at right-back – was determined
to make an impact. When the ball went out for a
throw-in on the far side, he allowed himself a couple
of seconds to look around the pitch and savour the
moment. This was really happening!

*

That summer, as he sat outside and enjoyed a family
barbeque, Sergio was glad of the rest. It had been a
whirlwind year.

'If I'd told you a year ago that you would soon
be making your debut for the first team, would you
have believed me?' René asked.

'No chance,' Sergio replied, laughing. 'I'd have
thought you were crazy. But the coaches have faith
in me, and I think next season could be a really big
one for me.'

No matter what he did, he couldn't take his mind
off football. Even a short holiday didn't do the trick.
All he wanted was to be in the gym and out on the
pitch working on his game.

When pre-season finally rolled round, Sergio

immediately stood out as being one of the best.

'He looks stronger, fitter and more confident,' one of the assistants pointed out.

The others agreed. 'Sergio has done everything we've asked. I think it's time to throw him into the deep end and start him at right-back this season.'

CHAPTER 8

BERNABÉU BOUND

Sergio's first full season in La Liga flew by, with the club finishing sixth. He surprised himself with how quickly he adapted to life as a pro – and people were taking notice. One morning as he walked out to his car after training, his phone rang. It was Luis Aragonés, the Spanish national team manager, or '*El Sabio*' ('The Wise Man') as most people called him.

For a split second, Sergio thought it might be a prank from one of his teammates, but he recognised the manager's voice.

'I'll keep it short, Sergio,' he said. 'We've picked you in the squad for the friendly against China next month. You've had a terrific season and we believe you'll be playing for Spain for many years to come.'

Sergio was speechless for a moment. 'Wow, that's amazing news,' he said. 'Thank you. I won't let you down.'

He didn't even have time to call all his family and friends before the news broke. On his drive home, his phone pinged again and again with new text messages.

Sergio's mum burst into tears as soon as he called his parents to tell them the news, while he could feel his dad's pride through the phone. 'It feels like only yesterday that we were watching the '92 Olympics together and imagining what it would be like if one of our children was part of it,' he said.

When Sergio joined up with the squad in Salamanca, he was as nervous as he could ever remember being. He was training with the some of the same players he had grown up idolising, and he was thankful that he got a warm welcome from them all.

On game day, he walked into the dressing room

before the warm-up and froze on the spot. The
famous red shirts were hanging all around the
dressing room and in the back corner, he saw his
name on one of them: RAMOS. He had always loved
playing for his country at youth levels – and that
pride was multiplied by a hundred for the senior
team. He took a photo on his phone and sent it to all
his family with a simple caption: 'Blessed'.

After a national anthem that made his whole body
tingle, he jogged over to his position at right-back
and did a few final stretches. 'This is so crazy,' he
thought to himself. He had a few loose touches early
on, but the jitters soon passed, and he played his part
in a 3–0 win. Before they left the dressing room,
his teammates all signed his shirt, which made it a
prized souvenir for the rest of his life.

*

Back at Sevilla, the fans had fallen in love with Sergio
– his physical style, his tough tackling and his bold
forward runs. Many already saw him as a future club
captain. But the mighty Real Madrid had other ideas.

They were tracking him closely as they tried to turn their fortunes around ahead of the 2005/06 season, and that meant some difficult conversations for the club's President, Florentino Pérez.

'We've got to do something about our defence,' one senior Real Madrid advisor explained. 'Even with all our Galácticos, we can't win every game 5–4.'

The room went quiet. Signing defenders was always a touchy subject.

'Look, I know it's not the flashy approach we're known for, but it's the only way forward,' the advisor continued, hoping to see nods around the table.

'But we've talked for months about signing a striker,' Pérez replied. 'Attacking football is what people think of with Real Madrid and we have a long history to protect.'

The conversation eventually shifted to which defenders might be available, and there was discussion about the pros and cons of each.

'Sergio Ramos at Sevilla is an interesting option

too,' Pérez said suddenly. 'He's only nineteen, but the boy can play. He loves to get forward too.'

There were nods as he said this and then everyone tried to talk at once.

'But he's still a bit raw and a bit reckless,' said one voice. 'Don't we want someone who can contribute for us straight away?'

'If we're going to buy a defender, that's the kind of guy we want,' argued another. 'He's a winner.'

'Okay then,' Pérez interrupted. 'We'll check on him and see what it would take to bring him here.'

'He's got a buyout clause with Sevilla,' a director explained. 'That should help us.'

Sergio had been in the league long enough to know that rumours could appear out of the blue, with no facts behind them. But he still gasped when he saw the report that Real Madrid were interested in signing him.

He called René, who had taken over as his agent and manager. 'I just saw the update. Real Madrid? Really? What's going on?'

'I was just about to call you. I'm trying to find

out if there's any truth to it, just to be prepared.
The ball would be in Sevilla's court though. You're
still under contract.'

'Okay, cool. Keep me posted.'

Sergio tried not to think about it. After all, he
loved life at Sevilla, and everyone had been so
supportive... but this was Real Madrid. Or at
least it *might* be Real Madrid. He found himself
daydreaming about playing in that famous white
shirt at the Bernabéu.

When René called back later that day, he
confirmed that conversations were underway
between the two clubs. 'Your release clause is
€27 million. We just have to wait and see whether
Real Madrid are willing to pay it.'

Sergio could hardly believe it. That would make
him the most expensive Spanish defender... *ever!*

With his head still spinning, Sergio hoped that
things would be decided quickly, one way or the
other. Sevilla president José María del Nido knew
that Sergio was the type of young talent that would
fit in at any big club and make an impact. He was

determined to demand a fair price that could help the Sevilla team rebuild itself.

'There's not much we can do to push this forward,' René explained as the negotiations rolled on. 'Just be patient. My gut tells me a deal will eventually happen.'

In the meantime, Sergio was trapped. He saw his face on every sports show and every newspaper. The gym was one of the few places where he could find some peace and quiet, but the idea of letting down the Sevilla fans caused his stomach to constantly ache.

Finally, he got the call from René. 'Sergio, we're still sorting a few final things, but the deal is going through. Just wanted you to know. I can say it out loud now – my brother is going to be playing for Real Madrid!'

Sergio felt a strange mix of happiness, relief and sadness. This was an incredible opportunity to make his mark at one of the world's biggest clubs, but it was Sevilla who had given him his chance as a professional.

After the meetings, René went straight to see Sergio.

'Little bro,' said René, 'do you realise that you are the only Spanish player that Florentino Pérez has signed in the past few years? Real Madrid really fought for you.'

Sergio half-smiled and nodded.

'What's wrong?' René asked. 'I thought we'd be celebrating tonight.'

'I'm excited,' Sergio said. 'I really am. But it's tough to turn my back on Sevilla.'

René nodded. 'I get it. But think of it this way, they got a huge transfer fee for you. That sets Sevilla up for years to come – all because of you.'

'Hmmm, I hadn't thought of it like that,' Sergio replied.

'And what reasonable fan could really blame you for being happy about signing for Real Madrid?'

Sergio laughed. 'I bet there are a few. Even some of my friends, I guess. But you're right. This is a special moment and I'm ruining it by being moody. Let's go see Mum and Dad and celebrate the news together.'

Pérez called Sergio an hour later. 'Welcome to
Real Madrid, Sergio!' he said. 'We can't wait to see
you at the Bernabéu for the press conference. For
now, I wanted to ask if you were happy with the
Number 4 shirt. It has a special place in our history
and Fernando Hierro has just retired. We think
you're the kind of player who can follow in those
footsteps.'

'This all still feels like a dream if I'm being
completely honest,' Sergio said. 'But, yes, Number 4
sounds great.'

'Great, we'll have that ready for the press
conference.'

They went through all the arrangements for
travelling to Madrid for Sergio's medical. He did
his best to follow the conversation, but a thousand
thoughts were flying through his head. He grabbed
a sheet of paper and scribbled some notes so he
would remember the key points.

Sergio had seen the videos of other players joining
Real Madrid, but those were superstars like Zinedine
Zidane and David Beckham. He did not expect many

people to show up for his introduction, but he was stunned to see huge crowds to welcome him.

'Sergio! Sergio! We love you!'

'You're the man to put us back on top!'

The day flew by, with questions, camera flashes and lots of smiling. When he finally got back to his hotel, he turned on the TV but fell asleep on the sofa before he could even choose a film to watch.

'There's so much still to do,' he told Miriam the next morning as he packed up to come home. 'But the club has booked the same hotel for me for the first few months so I can slowly start looking for a place to live.'

'We're here to help too. I can come up for a weekend and help you settle in.'

José María and Paqui couldn't let Sergio leave without a big party. They called cousins, aunts, uncles, friends and neighbours, and the back garden was full of familiar faces when Sergio arrived. 'You told me it was just a few friends!' he said to his mum, laughing. 'At least I know I've got a few fans here even I'm a flop at Real Madrid!'

CHAPTER 9

GETTING ON WITH THE GALÁCTICOS

When the first day of Real Madrid's pre-season training arrived, Sergio felt a different energy – the car park had been deserted when he dropped in for his medical; now there were fancy cars everywhere. The Galácticos were in the building!

Sergio vaguely remembered his way around and found the dressing room without too many wrong turns. He tried not to stare as he walked in, keeping his head down and finding his training kit neatly lined up at his locker. But once he sat down it was impossible not to watch what was going on around him.

To his left, Beckham and Zidane were looking at new Adidas boots that had just been delivered for

them to try out. To his right, Roberto Carlos and
Ronaldo were swapping stories with Robinho, another
summer signing. Opposite him, Raúl, Iker Casillas and
Michel Salgado were planning a pre-season party.

Somehow, Sergio was now part of this scene. At
least he already knew some of the Spanish players.

Iker spotted him and guessed that he might be
a little nervous. Rather than shouting across the
dressing room and putting all eyes on Sergio, he just
walked over and gave him a big hug.

'Hey Sergio, welcome to Real Madrid. It's great to
see you – I've been waiting for the club to put some
decent defenders in front of me!'

Michel came over to give Iker a playful jab in the
ribs. 'I heard that!' He shook hands with Sergio.
'Come and meet the rest of the lads.'

'We needed another Spaniard around here,' Raúl
said with a big grin. 'We can't have the Brazilians
running the place.'

Everyone laughed, especially Ronaldo and Roberto
Carlos, who both came over and put an arm on
Sergio's shoulder.

'You'll love it here,' said Ronaldo.

Sergio smiled and remembered his mum's words as he left the house to travel to Madrid. 'Don't be shy. I'm sure they're all just regular guys away from the cameras.' She was right.

Later that week, his family arrived in Madrid to spend a few days with him. All they wanted to know about was life with the Galácticos. Luckily, he had no shortage of stories. Being around some of the greatest players ever was never dull, and the flicks and tricks he saw in training were unlike anything he could even dream of trying.

'Remember how we used to make fantasy football teams with all the best players?' René said. 'Now you're playing on one of those teams!'

But after feeling starstruck for the first two training sessions, Sergio knew that he would never play his best football if he was constantly thinking of his teammates as superstars and heroes. Instead, he had to think of them as equals. After all, Real Madrid had paid €27 million to sign him; didn't that make him a Galáctico too? Okay, so Sergio didn't score goals like Ronaldo or bend the ball like Beckham, but he was unbeatable at the back. He was the future of the Real defence and it was time to show it.

'Get stuck in,' manager Vanderlei Luxemburgo told him one morning. 'The Galácticos may not always like it, but they'll respect it.'

'Sergio, remember, if you can keep Ronaldo and Raúl quiet in training, the rest of La Liga will feel like a walk in the park,' Iker added.

Once he brought that mindset, life was easier. He was calmer in the passing drills and less afraid to mark them in attack vs defence sessions. By the time the season kicked off, Sergio felt at home. He would probably never be a Galáctico, but he was certainly ready to wear the famous Real Madrid shirt.

But the first few months were a struggle. After one particular low point, Sergio stomped back to the dressing room and sat with his hands over his face. He was furious – partly with the referee but mostly with himself. He had just picked up his third red card of the season and it was only late November.

His first season with Real Madrid was in danger of becoming a nightmare.

How did this keep happening? Today it had been a split-second mistake: he lunged in when he felt confident that he could get the ball. It was a silly decision, especially as he already had a yellow card. When would he learn?

'Chin up, pal,' one of the assistant coaches told Sergio after jogging back to check on him. 'You were unlucky on that one but sometimes you've got to stay on your feet. Think about how Paolo Maldini and Fabio Cannavaro defend.'

Sergio nodded, still staring at the ground. 'It's just been a tough season with all the pressure. I'm a better player than I've shown so far.'

'Don't worry about that,' said the assistant coach. 'Everyone loves you and knows how talented you are. Don't be too hard on yourself. You're still only nineteen.'

Even with all the Galácticos, Real Madrid had a hard time gelling. Having played at right-back for Sevilla, Sergio was sometimes asked to play at centre-back and that was a whole new learning curve.

The 2005/06 season ended in disappointment for Real Madrid and there were plenty of questions from impatient voices inside and outside the club. Sergio had been thrown into a tough situation but, despite some wobbles, he was still standing. That counted as a victory.

'I think Real Madrid knew that my first year would be a bit of a roller coaster,' Sergio told his family after the final game of the season. 'But they've shown faith in me and now I have to prove them right.'

While a few of his teammates prepared for a long summer holiday, Sergio had other plans. A call from El Sabio confirmed that he had been chosen for the Spanish squad for the 2006 World Cup, and would be on the plane to Germany.

'Now I know this is going to be the year that Spain finally win again!' Paqui said proudly when she heard the news. 'Congratulations, darling. I feel better about our chances if *you're* in the squad.'

Sergio laughed. 'You're a bit biased, Mum, but I hope you're right!'

CHAPTER 10

SPAIN'S 'SPECIAL SOMETHING'

From Spain's first practice session when they arrived at their World Cup camp in Germany, El Sabio gave strong hints that Sergio would be starting at right-back, with Carles Puyol and Pablo Ibáñez in the centre. When they lined up for a practice match, Sergio was put with Xavi, Andrés, Iker and the rest of the usual starters.

'I don't want to jinx it, but I think I'm going to be starting,' Sergio whispered down the phone from his hotel room. He had to tell his parents, but didn't want anyone to overhear.

The reply from the phone echoed louder than his whisper. 'Wooooooooooooooooooooo!'

Sergio laughed. 'It's hard to believe, really. I only made my debut for the senior team a year ago. Now I'm at the World Cup!'

'Sergio, you keep thinking that this season was a disappointment, but you had some great games,' José María explained. 'You belong on the big stage and I know you'll prove that over the next few weeks.'

Sergio felt butterflies in his stomach as he thought about all the people back home who would be glued to their TV screens, cheering him on – his family, his school friends, maybe even his old teacher, Señor Nunez. But at the same time, this whole adventure with Spain had been such a whirlwind that he didn't have time to get too nervous. He believed in himself and he was ready to just let things unfold.

Before the kick-off of Spain's opening game, against Ukraine, Sergio went through his usual pre-match routine: the same food, taping his left ankle then his right, pulling on a sweatband for each wrist, and so on. As he walked down the tunnel and out into the electric atmosphere of a packed stadium, he still felt calm.

'Treat it as just another game,' he thought to himself.

It helped, of course, that he had already made his debut for Real Madrid at the noisy Bernabéu and experienced the El Clásico match against Barcelona. No match could ever be more intense than that.

After Spain and Ukraine's national anthems had played, Sergio passed the ball around with Carles Puyol and Xavi. Then he spotted El Sabio on the touchline waving for him to come over.

'Just play your natural, fearless game,' his manager told him. 'I've been around football long enough to know when a player has that special something. You were born to do this.'

Sergio jogged away with a huge smile on his face. He was ready.

Spain got off to a flying start, with two goals inside the first twenty minutes. That settled everyone down and they passed the ball around effortlessly. With all eyes on the Spanish midfielders' dazzling touches, there was plenty of room for Sergio to push forward. Again and again, he raced down the right wing to support the attack. The game finished 4–0 and the dressing room afterwards was buzzing.

'Great game today,' Iker said, patting Sergio on the back. 'You would never have guessed it was your first World Cup game.'

'That's the beauty of being a young player,' Raúl added. 'You just go out and play. You don't feel the pressure or have the bad memories that some of us old guys do!'

A 3–1 win over Tunisia kept Spain's momentum going and Sergio joined most of the other starters on the bench for the final group game against Saudi Arabia, with qualification already in the bag. Even that was a cool experience as he sat next to Xavi and Xabi Alonso and listened to them break down things in the game that he hadn't even noticed.

A powerhouse French team awaited them in the second round and it was hard not to feel a little intimidated. Sergio could remember watching Spain lose to France in the Euro 2000 quarter-finals. This time, though, *Les Bleus* had Thierry Henry up front, as well as Zidane pulling the strings as the playmaker. Sergio was both excited and a little anxious about trying to keep those two quiet.

Everything went according to plan for most of the first half. Early on, Sergio used his speed to beat Henry to the ball and clear the danger. He wasn't going to let anyone get past him without a fight. Then, in the twenty-eighth minute, David Villa put Spain ahead from the penalty spot. *1–0!*

'Come on!' Sergio screamed, punching the air with passion.

Just before half-time, however, France came powering back. Franck Ribéry beat the offside trap and then dribbled around Casillas. *1–1!*

In the second half, France pushed forward in search of a winning goal. Ribéry dribbled in off the right wing and crossed towards Eric Abidal at the back post, but Sergio stretched out his leg just in time to kick the ball away.

'Great defending!' Casillas clapped and cheered on his goal line.

Could Spain stay strong and win it? With ten minutes to go, Zidane curled a beautiful free kick towards Patrick Vieira at the back post. As he headed it goalwards, Sergio jumped up bravely to make the block, but he could only deflect the ball into his own net. *2–1 to France!*

Sergio's heart sank as he stood there gripping the goalpost. After all their hard work, was that game – and tournament – over for *La Roja*? Yes, it was – in injury time, Zidane scored a third on the counter-attack, while Sergio was up the other end, trying to equalise. Spain were out of the 2006 World Cup and were heading home.

At the final whistle, Sergio was devastated, but Zidane came over to comfort him.

'Hey, you should be really proud of your performance tonight,' his Real Madrid teammate told him. 'You'll be back in four years' time, I promise, and by then, you'll be the leader!'

Sergio tried his best to smile and look forward to that future. It took a few days for him to turn the page on the 2006 World Cup and refocus on Real Madrid. But by the time he was back on the training ground with the rest of the players, he felt great.

Despite catching the eye with his performances in Germany, Sergio hadn't forgotten that he still had work to do to prove himself at the Bernabéu.

By the end of the 2006/07 season, he had done just that. Real Madrid and Barcelona finished the season tied on seventy-six points, but Real clinched the league title because they had a better head-to-head record against their rivals. And Sergio had played a key part in both legs of *El Clásico*.

At home at the Bernabéu, he raced down the right wing and delivered a perfect cross to Raúl. *1–0!*

Then away at the Nou Camp, he out-jumped his Spanish teammate Carles to score with a fantastic flick header. *3–2!*

Goooooooooooooooooooooaaaaaaaaaaaaaaaaaalllllllllllll lllllllllllllll!!!!!!!!!!!!!!!!!!!

So, Sergio had certainly earned his first taste of La Liga glory and boy – did he enjoy the big celebrations at the Bernabéu. Real's Galácticos played like superstars and they partied like superstars too!

It had been a long season, but it was all worth it to be able to hold that huge trophy in his hands. Sergio still left manager Fabio Capello pulling his hair out a few times on the touchline because of badly timed tackles, but his manager was always quick to tell him to keep playing with his physical style.

Just to show it was no fluke, Real Madrid defended their title the following year. And this time, they were ahead of Barcelona by a massive eighteen points. By now, Sergio was one of their star players and a real fan favourite. That was because as well as winning lots of heroic headers and tackles at the back, he also loved to attack, scoring six goals a season. Not bad for a defender!

'Hearing them sing my name, just like they did at Sevilla, is an amazing feeling,' he told Miriam when she visited him. 'I'm one of them now. A true Madridista.'

'You've given them two straight championships,' she replied. 'I'd be singing your name too if I were a Real Madrid fan...'

Sergio gave her a jokey glare.

'...which I am, of course,' Miriam finished, laughing.

CHAPTER 11

EURO 2008: EXCITING NEW ERA

'Can you believe the boos?' Sergio asked, turning to Iker as they got changed after their last warm-up game before Euro 2008. 'We really need the fans to get behind us.'

'The fans are just so hungry for success at one of these tournaments,' Iker replied. 'I can't really blame them.'

Something felt different from the moment that Sergio joined up with his Spain teammates ahead of Euro 2008, to be hosted by Austria and Switzerland. He was still finding his way in international football, but he had already played enough times for his

country to notice the more positive feeling around
the squad.

El Sabio even lightened the training schedule,
cancelling one session so that the players could have
an afternoon off.

'Sergio, spread the word, we're having a video
game tournament in my room,' Xavi announced.
'Sounds like we'll have nine or ten guys there.'
Sergio thought back to the World Cup two years
earlier and couldn't remember anything like that
happening.

Ahead of Spain's first Euro 2008 game, El Sabio
gathered the players in one of the hotel meeting
rooms. 'We all know that other tournaments have
ended badly for us. If people want to write us off,
that's fine. Let them. This time, it's going to be
different. We're here to win.'

Spain looked deadly up front with Fernando
Torres partnering David Villa, and Xavi and Andrés
Iniesta pulling the strings. 'If we can just keep
things tight at the back, we'll be unstoppable going
forward,' Sergio had told his friends before leaving

for Austria. 'Whatever you do, don't make any plans for July.'

When the Spain bus arrived at the stadium for their first group game against Russia, Sergio could feel the nervous excitement building.

El Sabio gave the team their final instructions – 'Stick together, trust each other and be ruthless' – and Sergio joined in the high fives. 'Vamos!' the players screamed as they headed for the tunnel.

Playing at right-back, Sergio had countless chances to get forward and support the attack. If anything, he had to remind himself to stay back at times to avoid being caught out by quick Russian counter-attacks.

But once Spain got ahead, everyone could relax. Fernando raced onto a long pass and set up David for the first goal, and Sergio sprinted over to join the celebrations. 'Yes!!!'

David finished with a hat-trick, giving Spain the perfect start. The positive performance made the Spanish camp even more fun. 'Remember how we'd all just stick in small groups or stay in our own rooms at other tournaments?' Iker said one evening. 'Now, we've got most of the squad packed into one hotel room and it feels like we're all one big family!'

Spain picked up a second victory against Sweden, but this one felt a little sourer for Sergio. In the first half, he chased back to reach a dangerous through-ball but was muscled off the ball by Zlatan Ibrahimović for Sweden's equaliser. Sergio picked himself up off the floor, looked hopefully for a whistle or an assistant referee's flag, and then hung his head in disappointment.

'Brush it off, mate,' Iker called out. 'We'll just get another goal.'

David rescued Sergio with a last-minute winner, but that was not the end of it. El Sabio took Sergio aside at the next training session to deliver a bit of a wake-up call.

'Sergio, you're a huge part of this team but I need to see more focus. That doesn't just mean being in the right place on the pitch. It's also about showing up on time for meetings and doing all the little things that contribute to winning.'

Sergio was shocked – he knew he should have done better on the Sweden goal, but he had not realised that other factors were frustrating El Sabio.

He nodded, and El Sabio put an arm round his shoulder, eager not to leave Sergio too shaken.

'Message received,' Sergio replied. 'I'm desperate to win and I'll work even harder to help us bring home the trophy.'

Sergio had a few days to think things over as El Sabio rested his first-teamers in the final group game, with qualification already secured, but he was back for a tense quarter-final against Italy. As the match went to penalties, Sergio took a deep breath. He was not going to be one of the five penalty takers, but he might be called upon if it went to sudden death. He could barely watch as he lined up along the halfway line with his teammates. 'Come on, Iker!' he muttered under his breath.

It was a rollercoaster of emotions – joy as Iker saved one penalty, agony as Dani missed, then the joy of Iker making another big save. As Cesc Fàbregas stepped forward to take Spain's fifth

penalty, Sergio screamed encouragement. The
penalty flew into the net. Shootouts had been cruel
to the Spaniards in the past – but maybe this was a
sign that things were about to change.

Sergio sprinted over to Iker as most of the players
ran to Cesc, then they all gathered in one big huddle
to celebrate. 'Two more to go!' they chanted.

'We'll have to play better if we're going to beat
Russia in the semi-finals,' El Sabio reminded his
players. 'But enjoy this moment – we've certainly
waited long enough to win a shootout! I'm proud of
you guys.'

Sergio knew that the Russians would make a
fast start, spurred on by the loss to Spain earlier in
the tournament. El Sabio had talked a lot over the
last few days about getting through the first fifteen
minutes of a game without taking too many risks.
Mission accomplished – against the Russian team,
they got to half-time at 0–0, but would have to
finish the job without David, who had limped off.

Once Xavi scored early in the second half, Russia
never looked like recovering. Fernando almost

doubled the lead from Sergio's cross, and Spain
cruised to a 3–0 win. Back in the dressing room,
there was some singing and plenty of hugging, but
they all knew that the job wasn't done yet.

'The trophy is within reach now, boys,' Iker said
as they all sat at their lockers. 'We need ninety more
top quality minutes if we're going to beat Germany
in the final.'

Before he knew it, Sergio was on the bus on the
way to the final. As some of his teammates headed
out for the warm-up, he grabbed a marker pen and
prepared a message for his white undershirt. If he
was going to be celebrating at the final whistle, he
wanted everyone to know that Antonio was there in
his thoughts. His good friend from Sevilla had died
a year ago and Sergio still missed him. He would
never forget Antonio and all the moments they had
shared along the way.

El Sabio called for quiet and looked around the
dressing room. 'Our country has waited years for a
champion, and you have the chance to be part of
history today,' he said, almost shouting. 'But the

only way to do that is through togetherness. We're better than them man-for-man – I believe that, and you should too. But it's teamwork and courage that will get us over the line tonight.'

Those words had the right effect on Sergio. He was ready to run through a wall for his manager. He pulled up his socks, re-tied his boots and did a lap of the dressing room, high-fiving his teammates. As he stood in the tunnel, he pictured what it would be like to parade through the streets of Madrid if they won. Then he quickly snapped out of it. He was thinking too far ahead – and Germany were fearsome opponents.

Sergio sang the anthem loudly and proudly. His dad's words from earlier that day echoed in his mind. 'I know it's a huge moment in your career but try to enjoy it. I hope it isn't your only final for Spain, but it could be. Take it all in.'

He looked to his left and then to his right, and he saw large sections of red in the crowd. We're going to need the fans to push us along today, he thought.

Sergio saved his best game of the tournament for

the final. He had expected to be battling through aches and pains, but instead he felt fresh. While always making sure he didn't leave Carles stranded, he burst forward at every opportunity. Halfway through the first half, Sergio played the ball up the line to Cesc and then raced up in support. Cesc laid the ball back and Sergio clipped a perfect cross towards Fernando, whose header bounced back off the post.

Sergio jumped in the air expecting to see the ball end up in the net but could only put his head in his hands and run back to his position.

Fernando was more clinical ten minutes later, clipping the ball into the German net from Xavi's cross. *1–0 to Spain!*

'I was cursing you ten minutes ago but you're my hero again now,' Sergio joked as he hugged Fernando and jogged back to the halfway line.

'Keep the ball, keep the ball,' Xavi called as he floated around the pitch. Whenever Sergio was under pressure, Xavi was there for a quick pass. He never wastes a pass, Sergio thought to himself for the hundredth time that month.

Spain won a free kick midway through the second half, and Sergio looked to Carles to see who was going up for it. 'You go,' Carles replied.

Sergio drifted towards the back post and looked across to make sure he stayed onside. Xavi whipped the ball in and Sergio's eyes lit up. It was coming straight to him and he was unmarked. He watched it all the way and then powered a header towards the top corner. He looked up to see the German keeper tip the ball away at full stretch.

So close! The sea of red shirts behind the goal had jumped out of their seats ready to celebrate.

'I should have gone for the other corner,' he said to Xavi as he sprinted back, shaking his head.

Spain wasted a couple more chances, setting up a nervous last few minutes. Sergio never stopped running. He was still bursting towards the German box in the dying minutes, even as El Sabio was out on the touchline urging his team to stay calm.

Deep in stoppage time, Iker blasted a free kick up the pitch and the referee blew the final whistle. Spain were the new European Champions! Sergio rushed to his teammates as they hugged, jumped, screamed and sang. It was a summer he would never forget – and, for Spain, it was really just the beginning.

Campeones, Campeones, Olé, Olé, Olé!

CHAPTER 12

LOSING BATTLES WITH BARCELONA

'Turn it off,' Sergio called to René as they sat in his living room, watching Barcelona celebrate with the Champions League trophy. Red and blue confetti was scattered on the pitch and the players were halfway through a victory lap. 'I can't watch any more of this.'

René knew better than to argue. He reached for the remote and the room went quiet. Sergio stared at the floor.

'Don't get me wrong,' he said eventually. 'I'm happy for Xavi and Andrés. I love those guys. But all anyone wants to talk about is Barcelona. What about Real Madrid? People are forgetting all about us.'

It had been a tough year for the Galácticos. When they won La Liga in 2007 and 2008, all the talk was about Real Madrid. But they had been blown away by Barcelona during the 2008/09 season. Led by Lionel Messi, Barcelona had now landed the Treble. Guardiola, Sergio's old Olympics hero, had made history in his first season as Barcelona boss.

'We should all be watching this and getting angry,' Sergio said. 'If we need a reason to be doing extra training and fighting even harder, this is it. Barcelona have raised the bar. Now we have to respond. We better get things right next season, or the fans are going to be fuming.'

It didn't help that Real Madrid had been changing managers so regularly. Bernd Schuster was in charge for less than two seasons, then Juande Ramos lasted just six months. Now it was Manuel Pellegrini's turn.

As Sergio looked around the pitch during pre-season training, he was confident that Real Madrid had a squad capable of battling Barcelona all the way. They had top new players in every position: Raúl Albiol and Álvaro Arbeloa in defence, Xabi Alonso

and Kaká in midfield, and Karim Benzema and
Cristiano Ronaldo in attack.

The new Galácticos were ready to bounce back,
and the early signs were good:

Real Madrid	*3–2*	*Deportivo de La Coruña*
Espanyol	*0–3*	*Real Madrid*
Real Madrid	*5–0*	*Xerez*
Villarreal	*0–2*	*Real Madrid*
Real Madrid	*3–0*	*Tenerife...*

'We've won five out of five, we're scoring goals for
fun and we're keeping it tight at the back,' Sergio
told his parents one night. 'This is exactly the
response we needed.'

But Barcelona were always looming. When it
came to head-to-head battles, they always seemed
to have the edge. Sergio was up all night wondering
how Real Madrid had lost at the Nou Camp when
Barcelona played most of the second half with ten
men. It got worse when Barcelona won 2–0 at
the Bernabéu late in the season, with the Real

Madrid fans jeering Sergio and his teammates at the final whistle. Guardiola's men won the title by just three points.

'We can't beat them,' Sergio said to Iker, throwing his arms up in the air in frustration. They had also been through the pain of an early Champions League exit. 'That's another season without one of the big trophies. Now what? Another coaching change? No wonder the fans are booing us.'

Iker shook his head. 'I know, it's a rough spell for us at the moment. But you've just got to be patient – we all have to be patient. Our time will come again. We pushed Barcelona all the way in the title race. If the ball had bounced our way a couple more times, we'd be celebrating with the trophy now.'

'I know,' Sergio said, but he was still on edge. Iker got up to leave, thinking the conversation was over, but Sergio kept going: 'We have to stop trying to beat them at their own pretty passing game. It's not the Real Madrid way but maybe we have to be more physical and get in their heads. The trouble is, we're friends with half of their team!'

Iker laughed. 'Well, let's keep it that way. We're going to be travelling together to South Africa next week, so put your mind games on pause! Let's go and win the World Cup instead.'

CHAPTER 13

ON TOP OF THE WORLD

Sergio saw immediately that, after their success at Euro 2008, people were talking about Spain differently. For years, they had been the dark horses. Now, with the 2010 World Cup looming, they were being talked about among the favourites.

'That was just for starters,' Sergio told his mum as he packed his bag ready for the tournament in South Africa. 'We've got basically the same team and I don't think anyone, or anything, can stop us.'

He saw himself differently too. He had grown up a lot in the past two years and felt like a better defender and a better professional.

Spain were drawn in Group H alongside Switzerland, Honduras and Chile.

A nightmare start – a 1–0 loss to the Swiss – proved to be a wake-up call. 'Well, if you thought life would be easy as European champions, there's your answer,' said manager Vicente del Bosque, aka *El Mister,* to the shocked Spanish players in a very quiet dressing room. He was facing the tough task of following on from Aragonés's success at Euro 2008. 'But there's still time to put things right. We'll go over the film tomorrow and see what we need to fix. Let's make sure we're sharper against Honduras.'

Sergio was especially disappointed. He was one of the last to shower and get dressed afterwards. He knew Spain were much better than they had shown in that first game.

His dad called his hotel room that night to try to cheer him up. 'It's early days, son. I've watched enough of these tournaments to know that it's never over after one game.'

'We were terrible,' Sergio replied, with no energy

at all. 'That World Cup trophy feels a long way away right now.'

'You're talking like you're out of the tournament. Take it one game at a time. Go and win the next one.'

By the time the next game finally arrived, Sergio felt calmer and he wanted to make sure his teammates felt the same way. Luckily, he had a plan. He spoke to Iker that morning and explained what he needed him to do.

Two hours before kick-off against Honduras, as the players settled into their dressing room, Iker stood on a chair and waved his arms. 'Listen up, everyone. To help us get in the zone for today's match, we have a special guest DJ.'

Sergio peered through the doorway and saw Xavi, Andrés and Fernando looking at each other with confused faces. They were probably expecting a famous Spanish DJ, he thought, giggling to himself.

'Put your hands together for DJ Rockin' Ramos,' Iker announced.

Sergio put his sunglasses on and hit PLAY on his

music player. Music blared from the speakers tucked under his arm. He walked in and the dressing room erupted into cheers and laughter.

Iker high-fived him, while Sergio set up the speakers on the table in the middle of the room, and then asked, 'Who's ready for some classic Spanish tunes?' in his best DJ voice.

For some time, Sergio had been unofficially in charge of the music selection in the dressing room and on the bus. He hoped his little performance had taken some of the tension out of the pre-game build-up.

It seemed to work. Spain won 2–0 and the victory could have been even bigger. Sergio took every chance to get forward, seeing that Honduras posed little threat on the counter-attack. 'We were much better today,' he said to Iker as they walked back to the bus. 'Did you see the guy push me over in the box at that corner? We should have had two penalties. If the group comes down to goal difference, we might regret some of our misses, but we looked more like ourselves.'

'Yeah, I could probably have had a cup of tea and a picnic in the box tonight,' Iker replied. 'You guys didn't let them get near our goal.'

'If we take care of business against Chile, that sloppy start will be forgotten,' Sergio said.

Goals from David and Andrés were enough to sink Chile and put Spain top of Group H. That meant a matchup with Cristiano and Portugal in the next round. 'Get in!' Sergio shouted at the final whistle. 'We're back on track.' He never got tired of seeing the way David, Xavi and Andrés worked the ball around the pitch, even in the tightest spaces. 'Those guys give us a chance against anyone,' he had told René that morning.

As the bus pulled into the hotel where the Spanish squad was staying, Sergio's phone buzzed. It was a text from Cristiano. 'I'll try not to embarrass you too badly, but I can't promise anything!!'

Sergio laughed. Typical Cristiano. 'Make sure you bring your shin pads!' he wrote back.

Beneath all the jokes, Sergio knew the game against Portugal was going to be a tough battle and a game where he had to make defending the top priority. Vicente had a similar message. 'Normally, I'd say push up and give us that width on the right. But Cristiano is a different challenge. We can't leave that kind of space for him to hurt us.'

But with Cristiano spending more of his time on the other wing, the game plan changed a little. 'If he's on the other wing, we've got enough cover,' Vicente called as Sergio walked over to take a throw-in. 'You can be more aggressive in supporting the midfield.'

Sergio didn't need to be told twice. He pushed up, giving Andrés, Xabi and Xavi an outlet pass. With thirty minutes to go, he got the ball on the touchline, took a quick touch and swung in a dipping cross. It was perfect for Fernando, but his header was well saved. 'It's coming, boys,' Sergio shouted, with his hands still on his head after the near miss. Minutes later, David smashed the ball home after a quick-fire move. *1–0 to Spain!*

Sergio almost added a second goal late on with another burst down the right, hitting the ball as

sweetly as ever, but denied by another excellent
save. 'Oh, come on!' he yelled.

'That's your one good shot for the tournament
gone,' Andrés called, laughing.

The next round brought another narrow win in
a tournament full of low-scoring games. 'We're not
making things easy for ourselves,' Sergio said to
Miriam on their evening call after the 1–0 quarter-
final win over Paraguay. 'Thank goodness for Iker.
What a penalty save!'

'But we should have had a penalty too,' René
reminded him. 'Anyway, all that matters is that we
have a World Cup semi-final to look forward to
now. Germany will be out for revenge after the
Euro 2008 final.'

The build-up to the semi-final was eventful,
with Carles trying to fight off an injury and Sergio
wondering if he would have to shift over to centre-
back. 'I'll do whatever El Mister needs me to do, but
we need Puyi,' Sergio said to Iker as they waited for
the news. 'I've learned so much from him over the
past two tournaments.'

In the end, Carles was fit to start, giving Spain a big boost. 'We know how this tournament has gone,' El Mister said. 'Lots of cautious football and not many goals. When we get a chance, we've got to be ruthless. You know the Germans will be.'

El Mister's words rang true. Spain had plenty of the ball and passed it well, but it was 0–0 heading into the final twenty minutes. 'We just need one chance,' Sergio said to Carles as they waited for a German substitution.

Though Spain's midfield stars were small, they had four tall defenders capable of scoring from set-pieces. As Xavi put the ball down by the corner flag, Sergio joined Carles, Gerard Piqué and Joan in the box. Sergio made his burst towards the back post but saw instantly that the ball would not reach him. Instead, Carles came flying in and thumped a header into the net. *1–0 to Spain!*

'Puyi! What a header!' he screamed, chasing after him.

'World Cup final!' Sergio yelled as the final whistle sounded. Once again, one goal was enough for Spain.

The players hugged, the substitutes ran on to join in and Sergio could hear the fans going wild.

'Another clean sheet,' Iker said, patting Sergio on the back. 'One more of those and we could be world champs!'

Sergio had played in some big games, but the World Cup Final was on a whole other level. Only the Netherlands stood in their way, and Sergio knew all about their threats – Arjen Robben and Robin van Persie, in particular.

'To get this far and not lift the trophy would be too painful,' Sergio said, pacing his room while talking to Jesús Navas, who was now a regular in the Spain squad. 'We have to win.'

As they walked onto the pitch for the national anthems, they went past the glistening World Cup trophy. Sergio took a long look at the prize. 'We'll be back for you later,' he called out. He had stood with his teammates for the Spanish national anthem countless times, but this one was extra-special. The hairs stood up on his arms and the back of his neck.

The Dutch game plan was clearly to unsettle Spain

with a physical style of play. From the start, there were little trips and kicks. Sergio was one of the first to appeal to the referee when he saw Xabi hit the ground after a dangerous high foot. 'This is getting out of hand,' he said to Andrés after yet another foul.

Still, Spain just couldn't score – not in ninety minutes and not in 105 minutes. Sergio willed his body to keep moving as they entered the final five minutes of extra time. Then it happened. Sergio saw Jesús pick up the ball just in front of him and start a mazy dribble. Tired Dutch defenders struggled to keep up. The ball fell to Andrés in midfield, then out to Fernando on the left. 'Put it in the box,' Sergio yelled. Fernando's cross was only half-cleared, and the ball was scrambled through to Andrés. 'Shoot!' Sergio called, praying that this was the big moment. Andrés pulled back his right foot and rocketed in a low shot. *1–0!*

Sergio leapt in the air as he saw the net bulge. Everything else was a blur, from sprinting the length of the pitch, to joining the celebrations to surviving the remaining minutes. And then it was over. The

Dutch players threw themselves to the floor while Spain jumped for joy.

Climbing the steps to receive his medal took every last ounce of Sergio's energy, but it was an amazing moment that he would never forget. He was a world champion!

'I love this team,' he thought to himself as they posed for photos and sang with the fans.

Campeones, Campeones, Olé, Olé, Olé!

CHAPTER 14

THE MISKICK AND THE TRUCE

25 April 2012, Estadio Santiago Bernabéu, Madrid

Sergio carefully placed the ball on the penalty spot.
The Real Madrid fans fell silent, giving him a chance
to focus. He took a quick glance at Manuel Neuer
in the Bayern goal, charged in and struck the ball as
hard as he could. As soon as Sergio made contact,
he knew he was heading for disaster. He watched in
agony as the ball sailed high over the bar.

He turned angrily to look at the penalty spot, as if
it had somehow propelled the ball so high. It was an
ugly miss and he just couldn't believe it as he walked
slowly back to the halfway line. The crowd was in

shock. Thirty seconds later, the travelling Bayern fans were jumping around as they scored the winning penalty and clinched their place in the Champions League final.

Sergio was one of three Real Madrid players to miss in the shootout, and the other players and coaches tried their best to console him. But it really stung. After all the high points during the season, he felt like he had let everyone down.

He didn't want to talk about it either. He put a towel over his head and sat next to his locker. Meanwhile, he could hear the Bayern celebrations down the corridor.

Even winning La Liga a few weeks later could only slightly ease Sergio's pain of that penalty miss. Every time he thought he had moved on, it would pop up and upset him.

But the penalty miss wasn't the only thing on his mind when he came in to clear out his locker for the summer. As he and Iker sat down for lunch in the Real Madrid cafeteria, Sergio looked over his shoulder to check that they were alone and that there was no chance of manager José Mourinho walking in.

'This must be top secret stuff,' Iker replied. 'Wait, you're not being sold, are you?'

'No, nothing like that,' Sergio said, but his face stayed serious. 'We need to talk about this rivalry with Barcelona. It's getting out of hand. We have good friends on that team and there seems to be a red card every time we play them.'

Iker nodded. 'I know – and I think I can guess where you're going with this. We had some ugly games this season.'

It was Sergio's turn to nod. 'We're on the same page. How are we going to win Euro 2012 if we're not speaking to each other? We need to talk to Xavi and Andrés.'

'Do you think they'll pick up the call?'

'Come on, of course. We've been friends for years. I bet they are thinking the same thing that we are.'

With the room still quiet, Sergio took out his phone, dialled Xavi's number and hit the speakerphone button.

'Hey, man. It's Sergio and Iker. Listen, we were just talking about what a rough season this has been.

We're going to be on the same team at Euro 2012 and I think we need to clear the air.'

'I know,' Xavi said. 'We've been saying the same thing. I know it's an intense battle whenever Barcelona and Real Madrid play, but our friendship shouldn't get lost in that.'

'I'm really sorry for my role in the arguments,' Iker jumped in.

'Me too,' Sergio said.

'Thanks, guys. That means a lot. I know I got too fired up in one of the games as well. Let's start afresh when we meet up with the squad. We can forget all the nastiness of this season and focus on winning for Spain.'

'Awesome!' Sergio replied. 'Will you talk to Andrés too? We'll talk to the other Spanish boys here.'

'Cool, yes, I'll spread the word too. I think everyone will be glad not to turn up and be sitting on opposite sides of the room!'

They all laughed, mostly with relief.

'See you in a few weeks then,' Sergio said. 'Let's bring another trophy home.'

CHAPTER 15

EURO 2012: PLAYING IT COOL

By now, Sergio knew exactly what to bring for the big tournaments, and he expected to be at Euro 2012 all the way through to the final. As he was unpacking his suitcase, there was a knock at the door.

It was Iker.

'Seriously, you're still unpacking?' he said. 'I've never seen anyone take so long! Creams, hair gel, hand lotion – did you leave anything in your bathroom at home?'

Sergio laughed. 'Hey, some of us like to look our best for the cameras! What's wrong with that?'

Iker ignored that one. 'I'll wait for you and we can head down to the meeting together.'

He sat on the edge of the bed while Sergio found hangers for his last few T-shirts. 'We're on a mission to make history. Have you seen all the reports about that?'

'Yeah, they're everywhere at the moment,' Sergio replied. 'No team has ever won three in a row before. It would be pretty special to have six years at the top like that.'

'I really think we can do it, especially now that the team spirit has been repaired. We know how to pace ourselves and play our best football in the knockout rounds.'

All of that proved to be true as La Roja surged through to the semi-final against Portugal. It was the same old Spain, even if their defence was slightly different. Carles had injured his knee just weeks before the start of the tournament, and so Sergio had switched from right-back to centre-back, the position he usually played for Real Madrid. He was really enjoying his new role alongside Gerard at the heart of the backline.

Now, however, Sergio was facing another test

of his nerves. The semi-final had finished goalless
after extra time, which only meant one thing: a
penalty shootout. Just a couple of months after
his penalty heartbreak against Bayern, Sergio had
a choice to make – sit it out or put himself in the
spotlight again.

El Mister and his coaching staff were writing out
the names of the five Spanish penalty takers and
checking on any possible injuries that might affect
the order. When it came to Sergio, El Mister just
wanted to be sure.

'Sergio, what do you think? Still feeling
confident?'

Sergio had already made his decision. He was not
a quitter. 'One hundred per cent!'

'Okay, great. You've got the fourth penalty.'

When Sergio's turn came, there had already been
two misses, one for each team, and the shootout
was deadlocked at 2–2. He had the chance to put
Spain back in front. 'Good luck, pal,' Andrés said
quietly as Sergio started the long walk from the
halfway line.

Sergio placed the ball on the spot and took a deep breath. He knew exactly what he was going to do, and he had practised it again and again over the past week. Now he just had to get it right under pressure. He took eight steps back and then began his run up. At the last second, he pulled back from blasting his shot and just gave the ball the softest clip straight down the middle. As the Portugal keeper dived to his left, Sergio's penalty floated softly into the net.

'Vamoooooooos!' Sergio shouted, pointing to the Spain badge on his shirt.

He jogged back and rejoined his teammates on the halfway line.

'What a show-off!' teased Cesc. 'It takes nerves of steel to do that in a big semi-final.'

'Well, it turns out that hitting penalties as hard as I can doesn't end well for me!' Sergio replied, laughing.

Now they turned and begged Iker to come up with a big stop. Bruno Alves ran forward for Portugal's fourth penalty and his shot cannoned back off the bar.

That meant Cesc had the chance to win it. 'Come

on, come on, come on,' Sergio whispered under his breath. Cesc's shot went low to the left, and the keeper anticipated that correctly, but the ball hit the inside of the post and rolled into the opposite corner. Spain were in yet another final!

Cesc ran to Iker and the whole squad followed.

As Sergio walked back to the dressing room, he thought back to his Champions League penalty. It was a cruel way to decide games, but he was proud of himself for not shying away from it.

'A lot of players would have hidden in that moment,' El Mister told Sergio the next morning. 'Instead, you ran towards it. I haven't seen many more confident penalties than that one!'

'I'll always put my hand up for that kind of thing,' Sergio said, shrugging. 'The more pressure, the better. Bring it on.'

Sergio had heard some neutrals moaning about Spain being in another big final, but they had won games the easy way and the hard way, all while conceding just one goal. He took particular pride in that.

Spain had struggled to score goals during the tournament, but in the final they attacked Italy like a team that had been hiding those talents all along. Xavi and Andrés were everywhere. Sergio loved to watch that duo on top form. It was 2–0 at half-time and the Italians had barely had the ball. 'Don't relax, guys,' Sergio called out in the dressing room, sensing that his teammates were taking their foot off the gas. 'Let's keep the ball and get a third goal.'

The second half drifted along, and Sergio kept one eye on the clock on the scoreboard. Italy were running out of time and, as they sent more players forward, Spain put the finishing touches on another tournament victory. Fernando and Juan Mata, both on as subs, scored in the final ten minutes as Sergio got ready for yet another international victory lap.

As Iker lifted the trophy high above his head and Sergio jumped up and down with one arm around Xavi, the tension from the battles against Barcelona was the furthest thing from any of their minds. Spain had won their third straight major tournament. 'I'm not done yet,' Sergio told René as the players met up with their families. 'Now we've got to make it four in a row.'

René rolled his eyes and smiled. 'All that can wait. At least give yourself a few hours to savour this one. Come on, follow me. Mum and Dad are waiting to see the medal.'

CHAPTER 16

PILAR

Just like after the glory at Euro 2008 and the 2010
World Cup, Sergio and his teammates celebrated
their Euro 2012 success in style with a huge party
back in Spain. As he walked into the room in his best
suit, he had no idea that it was a night that would
change his life.

First, he had some familiar faces to catch up with.
He shook hands with old friends, former teammates
and former coaches. There was a smile on every face.
'Viva España!' one of them shouted.

Across the room, he spotted Ivan, a TV presenter
who he knew well from covering games with both
Real Madrid and Spain. Ivan waved, and Sergio

picked up his drink and walked over to catch up.

'I haven't seen you in months,' he said, giving Ivan a big hug.

'That's what happens when you're busy being famous and winning tournaments, I guess,' Ivan replied, along with a playful punch on the arm. 'By the way, we all loved that penalty!'

'Thanks,' Sergio said, laughing. 'If I'd messed it up, I would have been so embarrassed. It was a crazy summer – again – but it's good to be back and have a few weeks to go on holiday and...'

But Sergio didn't finish his sentence. Suddenly he was lost for words. A woman appeared next to Ivan with a drink in each hand. Sergio recognised her straight away.

Ivan turned, and took his drink. 'Thanks, Pilar. Cheers!' He paused. 'You've met Pilar before, right?'

Sergio shook his head. 'No. We've probably been at the same party a few times but we've never been introduced. I'm Sergio.'

He put out his hand and Pilar shook it.

'I know who you are!' she said, giggling. 'We've

all been watching you guys for the past month. Congratulations!'

Sergio went a bit red but recovered quickly. 'Thanks! I was just starting to tell Ivan that all I want to do now is sit on a beach for a few weeks.'

'Weren't you doing that in between the games at the Euros? All you had to do was play for ninety minutes and then you got three days off. I wish my job worked like that.'

Sergio was about to argue when he saw in her eyes that she was teasing him. She grinned, and he grinned back. 'You almost got me with that one,' he said.

Ivan's phone buzzed. He mouthed 'Sorry' and disappeared towards a quieter spot.

'Are you working tonight or are you just here for the party?' he asked. Pilar was a TV presenter and one of the most well-known women in the country.

'No work for me tonight,' she said. 'I'm meeting up with a couple of friends, but they're running late, so you've got me all to yourself for now.'

Sergio smiled. The more he talked to Pilar, the

more he felt a connection. The way she laughed took his breath away.

It turned out they had a lot in common, and Pilar spent most months in Madrid. Sergio really hoped that meant he might see her again in the weeks ahead.

Suddenly Pilar waved across the room. Her friends had arrived.

'Give me your phone for a minute,' she said.

Sergio handed it over hesitantly and watched as Pilar pressed a few different buttons. He hoped this wasn't some kind of joke.

'There you go,' she said, passing the phone back. 'My number is in there now. Give me a call if you want some company for your relaxing summer plans.' She gave him a kiss on the cheek and disappeared through the crowded room.

Sergio watched her go.

'I bet you're happy you came to the party now,' a voice said from behind him.

He turned to see Ivan looking very proud of himself.

'She's amazing,' Sergio said. 'I really want to see her again. This could be the start of something great.'

Soon, Sergio and Pilar were inseparable – long walks, fancy dinners and quiet nights in front of the TV. In no time at all, it felt like Pilar had been part of his life for years.

'I can't wait to see what's next for us,' he told Paqui that summer. 'I think she's the one.'

CHAPTER 17

LA DÉCIMA

'This is it, boys,' Sergio called, as the Real Madrid players filtered out towards the tunnel. 'Dig in for ninety minutes and we'll be back where we belong – in the Champions League final.'

'*La Décima*!' they all shouted. Real Madrid had been chasing their tenth European crown for years. If they could hold onto their 1–0 first leg lead against Bayern Munich, *La Décima!* would be at their fingertips.

As Sergio passed the ball back and forth with Luka and Pepe, he could feel the noise from the Bayern fans getting louder.

'Take no chances early on,' he reminded them. 'If

they get off to a fast start, this place will be rocking.'

Sergio did his best to set the tone, sticking tightly to Bayern strikers Mario Mandžukić and Thomas Müller. 'Don't let them get comfortable,' Real's latest manager Carlo Ancelotti had said again and again during the week.

As Real Madrid started to settle, they won a corner on the far side, and Sergio jogged forward. As usual, the penalty area was packed so he took a few steps out towards the edge of the box. Jinking one way, then the other, he tried to create some space to attack the cross. From his earliest days with Camas, he had been an expert at being in the right place at the right time for crosses.

Sergio spun away from his marker just as Luka swung the corner in and instantly saw it was a perfect ball. He just had to make the right connection. He timed his jump well and powered a header towards the goal. No goalkeeper could save that.

Gooooooooooooooooooooaaaaaaaaaaaaaaaalllllllllllll llllllllllllll!!!!!!!!!!!!!!!!!!!

Sergio sprinted off to celebrate and slid on his

knees near the corner flag. His teammates were
chasing after him in a flash. 'You little beauty!' Karim
screamed in his ear.

'We've got to finish the job now!' Sergio replied,
patting the Real Madrid badge on his shirt.

A few minutes later, Gareth Bale won a free kick
in a dangerous position and Sergio was back in the
Bayern box. Sergio signalled for Pepe to come over
and whispered, 'Make the near post run – it might
end up being a decoy, but you'll clear space for the
rest of us.'

When he saw Pepe dart towards the near post,
Sergio pulled behind him. Once again, the ball in
was a good one. Sergio saw Pepe leap and get a little
flick. There was no time to think – his instincts took
over. He dived forward to where he thought the ball
would land and timed it perfectly to guide a header
into the net.

*Gooooooooooooooooooooaaaaaaaaaaaaaaaaalllllllllllll
llllllllllllllll!!!!!!!!!!!!!!!!!!!!*

This one meant even more. Now the final really
felt within reach.

'Vamoooooooooooos!' Sergio yelled, pumping his fists. He couldn't believe he had scored two goals in a Champions League semi-final.

'You're a natural goalscorer,' Cristiano said, hugging Sergio.

'You guys have such an easy job,' Sergio joked. 'Just give me two chances and I'll score two goals.'

Cristiano scored a third before half-time and the Real Madrid dressing room was full of excitement. 'Don't lose your focus,' Carlo said, trying to keep his players grounded. 'Crazy things can happen if you start thinking the game is over. I'm sure you all remember my AC Milan team that was winning 3–0 at half-time and lost the 2005 final.'

With Sergio winning every header and every tackle, Bayern had no way back, and later on Cristiano completed a special night, making it 4–0.

Even having won so many big games, this one meant a lot. 'I'm going to remember this night for a long time,' Sergio told Luka. 'We ripped them apart.'

Luka grinned. 'You always save your best games for when we need them the most. When you scored the first goal, I knew we were going to be fine.'

'The biggest test is still to come,' Carlo warned. 'If we want *La Décima*, we will have to fight to the final second. But all that can wait. For now, let's enjoy tonight.'

The next three weeks went by slower than ever for Sergio. The final weeks of the La Liga ticked by and then it was all about the Champions League final – in Lisbon against cross-city rivals Atlético Madrid.

By the time he walked into the hotel meeting room for the team's final preparations, the semi-final victory felt like a whole season ago. 'We can't blow this chance,' he had told René on the phone that morning. 'We haven't won the Champions League for twelve years. For a giant club like this, that's unacceptable.'

Once all the players had grabbed some water and found a seat, Carlo went over the game plan. 'We know Atlético well, and they know us. This is going to be a tight, physical game and we have to stay calm. Atlético will pack the midfield and force us to beat them on the wings. Be direct.'

Sergio heard those words in his head again as he
walked out onto the pitch for the final, with the
Champions League anthem welcoming the teams.
That always gave him goosebumps.

Ten minutes before half-time, disaster struck for
Real Madrid. Atlético looped a ball back into the box,
Iker started to come out for it, then stopped, and
Atlético defender Diego Godin headed the ball into
the net. Sergio kicked the turf in anger.

The minutes ticked by in the second half. Sergio
clapped his hands to encourage his teammates and
did his best to drive forward with the ball when
Atlético sat back. He partly wished he was playing at
right-back so he could get forward more.

Gareth fired two shots wide, Cristiano mistimed
his jump for a header from Sergio's cross, and Isco
missed the target from just outside the box. The
prospect of *La Décima* was slipping away. 'There's
still time,' Sergio called to his teammates.

Deep into stoppage time, Real Madrid won a
corner on the right. Luka placed the ball by the
corner flag and took a deep breath. He had a quick

look at where he wanted to land the cross. Sergio
jumped on the spot, getting ready to attack the ball
if it came near him. Atlético defenders were grabbing
shirts and doing everything possible to deny a clean
header.

It was now or never. Sergio made a sharp run
and got in front of his marker. The ball was perfect.
He rose, almost in slow motion, and headed the
ball down towards the corner and past the keeper's
desperate dive.

*Goooooooooooooooooooaaaaaaaaaaaaaaaaalllllllllllll
llllllllllllll!!!!!!!!!!!!!!!!!!!*

Sergio had done it again.

The Real Madrid fans were on their feet – hugging
and cheering. Sergio threw himself on the ground
near the corner flag and his teammates dived on top.
Even the substitutes were running over to celebrate
with the hero of the hour.

'You're a lifesaver, man,' Cristiano said. 'What a
header!'

'We're not leaving here without *La Décima*,' Sergio
answered. He was so fired up that he felt dizzy.

He looked back at the Atlético players, who were picking themselves up off the ground. His joy was their heartbreak.

Carlo huddled the players together on the pitch as they prepared for extra time. There could surely only be one winner now, given Real Madrid's momentum. 'They're on the ropes and probably still in shock,' said Carlo. 'Play direct and run at them. There are going to be some tired legs out there.'

Sergio could see something was bothering Gareth. He walked over and put his hand on his shoulder. 'What's up, mate?'

'I can't hit the target today,' Gareth said, shaking his head. 'The game would be over if I'd taken my chances.'

'Come on, man. Don't worry about that. You're getting into the right positions and we all believe in you. Just focus on the next chance.'

Real Madrid were flying again. Luka raced forward but his shot was easily saved. Meanwhile, Cristiano had had a quiet game, but was now livening up.

'Keep attacking!' Sergio shouted, clapping his

hands. 'Another goal is coming. I can feel it.'

He was right. Ángel Di María weaved in and out
of back-pedalling defenders and his cross looped up
to the back post where Gareth jumped highest to
head the ball into the top corner.

'What a comeback!' Sergio yelled as he ran over
to celebrate. He jumped on Gareth's back. 'I knew
you'd get the next one!' he shouted.

Marcelo smashed in a third goal for Real Madrid,
and Sergio could see what it all meant to the fans.
Then it was Cristiano's turn. He dribbled into the
box, pushed the ball away from two defenders and
was tripped. Penalty!

'This will just be the icing on the cake,' Sergio
said, turning to Pepe as Cristiano stepped up to the
spot. 'What a night!'

Cristiano drilled home the penalty and now it
really was party time. Sergio sprinted across the pitch
to join the celebrations by the corner flag. '*Olé olé,
olé, olé,*' sang the Real Madrid fans.

Carlo embraced each of his players at the final
whistle but saved his biggest hug for Sergio. 'Big

players step up in big moments. You were a beast tonight.'

Sergio smiled. It was easily the most important goal he had ever scored.

As he walked over to high-five the rest of his teammates, he stopped to console the Atlético players who had seen their dream crushed. 'Neither team deserved to lose tonight,' he said. 'You guys had a great season. Be proud.'

One of the Real Madrid coaches suddenly appeared with a pile of T-shirts and started handing them out. Sergio unfolded his and saw a big Number 10 on the front – a special way to mark *La Décima* in all the photos with the trophy.

When it was Sergio's turned to hold the trophy, he took a long look at it. It had been a long quest, but he was finally a Champions League winner. He kissed it and raised it high in the air.

'Wooooooooooooooooooo!' the crowed cheered.

'What a feeling!' he shouted to Iker, who was standing next to him but could barely hear him with the crowd singing and music blaring.

'I know!' Iker called out. 'From Euro 2008 through to tonight, the last six years have been straight out of a fairytale book.'

'Let's hope there are a few more chapters left,' Sergio said, as he waved and blew kisses to the crowd.

CHAPTER 18

EL CAPITÁN

Sergio's life had been a whirlwind over the previous twelve months. He loved every part of it, but it was still exhausting. Pilar and their newborn son Sergio Jr. had turned his world upside down in the best possible way, and even the worst days didn't seem so bad anymore. As part of Spain's squad for the 2014 World Cup in Brazil, Sergio had been gloomy for a day or two when they were eliminated at group stage, but his family quickly had him smiling again. There was more to look forward to as well – Pilar was pregnant with baby number two.

One day, Sergio was sitting in his back garden, enjoying a rare summer break, when his phone buzzed. It was Pérez, the President of Real Madrid.

Sergio answered straight away. 'Hi Florentino. I thought you were on vacation.'

'I am, but I wanted to book a time to meet with you when I'm back. We need to finalise your new contract and I have a few other things to talk through.'

'Sure thing. I'm going to be at the Bernabéu with René next Thursday for a club event, so we can drop by then.'

When Sergio and René sat down in Florentino's office and took a sip of the water laid out for him, Pérez turned suddenly and said, 'Can you believe you've been a Real Madrid player for ten years now?'

'In some ways, it feels like it can't possibly be that long, but then I think about what has happened in my life, on and off the pitch, and I guess it makes sense. I'll always remember how you put your trust in me, even as a teenager.'

'I had a feeling, right from the start, that you were going to be a superstar. Then when you came in and started crunching Ronaldo and Raúl, I knew for sure.'

They all laughed.

'Well, let's start with the contract,' Pérez said, looking at both Sergio and René. 'We see you at the very centre of the next era at Real Madrid. Our offer reflects that. You don't have to sign anything today but see what you think.'

He leaned forward and passed across two folders with documents inside. Sergio and René read through the offer. René had coached Sergio years ago to keep a serious face in these meetings and not give away what he was thinking.

'It's clear that you value Sergio,' René said, closing his folder. 'Just give us a day or two to talk it over and we'll give you a firm answer.'

'Excellent,' Pérez replied. 'There's one other thing I want to cover today that is sort of linked to the contract offer.'

Sergio leaned forward in his seat, eager to hear more.

'Obviously, it was a tough blow to lose Iker to Porto this summer after all his years of service with Real Madrid but now we have to find a new club captain. We need someone who loves Real Madrid, has the respect of all his teammates and is a proven winner. We'd like it to be you.'

Sergio smiled and put his hands to his mouth. 'Wow, what an honour! Real Madrid captain – I like the sound of that.'

Pérez grinned. 'You're a natural leader and you've been setting an example for the boys for years now. It's time for you to take over the armband.'

As Sergio and René headed back to the car, they walked in silence. Once they set off driving, though, Sergio couldn't stay quiet any longer.

'That feeling of walking out at the Bernabéu as captain is going to be incredible,' he said.

'To be fair, it's a great contract offer too,' said René. 'We can take another look through it tonight, but I expect we can give Florentino a quick answer on that too.'

The next morning, Sergio called Florentino to give him the good news: yes and yes.

'Fantástico!' Florentino replied. Sergio could hear him tapping his desk in celebration. 'The next few years are going to be a lot of fun for Real Madrid.'

As Sergio played with Sergio Jr. at the park that afternoon, he was excited to have a few more weeks of family time before getting back into football mode, but equally he couldn't wait for the new era at Real Madrid to start.

CHAPTER 19

MORE SUCCESS WITH ZIZOU

When Sergio heard the news about the new Real Madrid manager, he hopped out of his seat and turned on the TV. It was official now – Zidane, who had worked with the players a lot when Carlo was in charge, was taking over.

'Is the bald guy in charge now?' Pilar asked, grinning.

'That's Zidane!' Sergio shot back. 'You can't call him that! But yes, he's the new boss.'

At training later that week, the new boss called Sergio aside. 'Did you ever think I'd be your manager one day when we were chasing trophies together?' Zizou joked.

Sergio laughed. 'I guess I thought you'd have your feet up at the beach when you retired.'

'I got bored of the quiet life pretty quickly, and I loved working with Carlo and you guys. It made me realise that I wanted to be in the hot seat eventually.'

'Well, this is going to be a fun ride. The boys are all really excited. Some of them had posters of you on their wall growing up.'

Zizou rolled his eyes. 'Thanks for making me feel like an old man!'

They carried on walking around the pitch as the training session continued around them.

'Listen, Sergio, we have a chance to do something really special here. We've got it all – a solid defence, midfield playmakers and deadly strikers. But it all starts with you. The players look up to you. When you talk, they listen. Together, we've got to keep everyone focused but give them the freedom to play the Real Madrid way.'

Sergio nodded. Zizou knew the club inside out and there was already a lot of talk about Real Madrid soon being back to their attacking best.

The consistent league form was still a work in progress that season, but Real Madrid's love affair with the Champions League continued as Zizou guided them back to the 2016 final. Just as in 2014, they would face Atlético. Sergio still got goosebumps when he thought about his last-minute header from two years earlier.

He felt confident as he led the team out for the final, and determined to get the team off to a good start. He never missed a chance to get into the box for corners and free kicks, and he jogged up to join Cristiano and Karim for a first-half set piece. The ball flew into the box through a sea of bodies and landed right at Sergio's feet. He reacted quickest and poked the ball into the net.

Goooooooooooooooooooooaaaaaaaaaaaaaaaaaalllllllllllll llllllllllllll!!!!!!!!!!!!!!!!!!!

But Atlético fought back, putting Sergio in the spotlight for yet another penalty shootout. As usual, he was the fourth taker, and he marched forward to pick up the ball and place it on the spot. The shootout was locked at 3–3. He took a moment

to steady himself, paused for a split second in his
run up to fool the keeper and then stroked the
ball into the bottom corner. He pumped his fist in
celebration. As the next Atlético penalty bounced
back off the post, Sergio was jumping up and
down. 'Come on, Cristiano. You've got this!' he
called out.

Cristiano made no mistake and Real Madrid
were champions again. Sergio threw himself
onto the pile of teammates already surrounding
Cristiano.

A year later, Zizou was still working his magic.
Real Madrid had reclaimed La Liga and were
back in the Champions League final again – this
time against Juventus. It was another tense first
half but Sergio watched from the back in admiration
as the Real Madrid midfield took over in the
second half.

The highlight of yet another magical European
night was a celebration on the pitch at the end,
for which Sergio was joined by his family: Pilar,
Sergio Jr. and the newest addition, Marco. Even

though Sergio was tired and sweaty, there was nothing better than sharing that moment with the people he loved most in the whole world.

Sergio thought back to what Iker had told him years before when Barcelona were the powerhouse of Spanish football. 'Our time will come,' Iker had said.

'I guess this is our time,' Sergio said to himself as the Real Madrid fans sang the players' names again and again.

With Zizou, there was no chance of taking things easy. He made that very clear when the squad arrived for the 2017/18 season. 'We're starting with a clean slate again. The Champions League wins count for nothing, and teams are going to be even more desperate to stop us, especially Barcelona. We can't let it slip now.'

Sergio led by example, demanding even more from his teammates. He had the authority to tell Cristiano to stop sulking, or to tell Luka to get more involved. They had been through so many battles together that the dressing room had a family feel.

Again, Real Madrid proved too strong in the knockout rounds, reaching a third consecutive Champions League final. 'There was a time when I couldn't picture winning even one Champions League title,' he told Pilar at breakfast the week before the 2018 final. 'Now, I have a chance to lift the trophy as captain for a third time.'

Pilar smiled. 'Well, we'll be there to cheer you on. It's funny, I've been trying to explain to Sergio Jr. that football isn't usually like this. He expects to see you in the final every year.'

Like the previous two finals, a familiar pattern emerged in 2018. Real Madrid scored first, had lots of the ball then had to regroup after a surprise equaliser. Liverpool were pressuring them all over the field and the game was hanging in the balance. 'Keep going, guys,' Sergio called out, clapping his hands. 'Move the ball, find the open man.'

Luka and Toni took back control in midfield – and then Zizou made the key change, bringing Gareth on. Minutes later, Gareth scored one of the best goals Sergio had ever seen – an unstoppable bicycle

kick into the top corner. Sergio punched the air.
They had one hand on the trophy.

When the final whistle finally arrived, it was a
familiar scene with Sergio at the centre of the party.
'I love you guys,' he told every teammate he could
find. 'Champions again!'

CHAPTER 20

THE ROAD AHEAD

Real Madrid's Champions League winning streak was foiled in the 2018/19 season, and Sergio could tell that another new era was approaching. One by one, his best friends had moved on: Iker had signed for Porto, and then his centre-back partner Pepe had joined Beşiktaş. Now, Cristiano had been sold to Juventus, and Sergio sensed that other players were looking for a new challenge.

After all, what else was there left for him to achieve at Real Madrid? From a raw and reckless nineteen-year-old right-back, he had gone on to become one of the deadliest defenders in the world, winning everything along the way: four La Liga titles, four

Champions League trophies, four FIFA Club World Cups, three UEFA Super Cups and two Spanish Cups.

And that was just at club level; Sergio had also won two European Championships and a World Cup with his country, Spain.

But despite all that success, at the age of thirty-three, Sergio was still learning lessons. He kicked himself for trying to work the Champions League yellow card rules in his favour. By getting booked in the Round of 16 first leg against Ajax, he thought it was a safe bet to miss the second leg and return for the next round. But Ajax stunned the Bernabéu with a 4–1 win as Sergio watched from the crowd. He could hardly believe what he was seeing.

As he looked to the future, Sergio knew there were plenty of options, but all that could wait. He had a summer ahead to enjoy with friends and family, and a chance to reflect on everything he had achieved in his career.

'Whatever comes next, it's sure to be a wild adventure,' Pilar said, putting her arms around him. 'Just follow your heart.'

Sergio smiled. As long as Pilar and the boys were with him, he couldn't go wrong.

With a beautiful red-and-orange sunset in front of him, Sergio turned to Pilar, René and his parents. 'I've been thinking a lot about everything you've all done for me along the way,' he said. 'I'm so thankful.'

René shook his head. 'No, we have to thank you as well. This journey has been so memorable for all of us. The little boy from Camas who signed for Real Madrid and won every trophy for club and country. What a story!'

Real Madrid

🏆 La Liga: 2006–07, 2007–08, 2011–12, 2016–17

🏆 Copa del Rey: 2010–11, 2013–14

🏆 Supercopa de España: 2008, 2012, 2017

🏆 UEFA Champions League: 2013–14, 2015–16, 2016–17, 2017–18

🏆 UEFA Super Cup: 2014, 2016, 2017

🏆 FIFA Club World Cup: 2014, 2016, 2017, 2018

Spain

🏆 UEFA European Under-19 Championship: 2004

🏆 UEFA European Championship: 2008, 2012

🏆 FIFA World Cup: 2010

Individual

🏆 La Liga Breakthrough Player of the Year: 2005

🏆 UEFA Team of the Year: 2008, 2012, 2013, 2014, 2015, 2016, 2017, 2018

🏆 FIFA World Cup Dream Team: 2010

🏆 UEFA Euro Team of the Tournament: 2012

🏆 La Liga Best Defender: 2011–12, 2012–13, 2013–14, 2014–15, 2016–17

🏆 UEFA Champions League Squad of the Season: 2013–14, 2015–16, 2016–17, 2017–18

🏆 La Liga Team of the Season: 2015–16

🏆 UEFA Defender of the Season: 2017, 2018

RAMOS

4 **THE FACTS**

NAME: SERGIO RAMOS GARCÍA

DATE OF BIRTH: 30 March 1986

AGE: 34

PLACE OF BIRTH: Camas

NATIONALITY: Spanish

BEST FRIEND: Cristiano Ronaldo

CURRENT CLUB: Real Madrid

POSITION: CB

THE STATS

Height (cm):	184
Club appearances:	685
Club goals:	94
Club trophies:	20
International appearances:	170
International goals:	21
International trophies:	3
Ballon d'Ors:	0

★ ★ ★ **HERO RATING: 87** ★ ★ ★

GREATEST MOMENTS

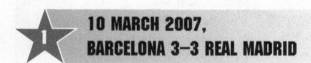

10 MARCH 2007, BARCELONA 3–3 REAL MADRID

After his €27 million move to Real Madrid, Sergio soon showed what a big game player he was. In this *El Clásico* match at Barcelona's Nou Camp stadium, he outjumped his Spain teammate Carles Puyol to score a fantastic flick header. Sergio's goal helped earn his team an important draw and two months later, he lifted the first of his four La Liga titles.

29 JUNE 2008,
GERMANY 0–1 SPAIN

Sergio played brilliantly as Spain's right-back at Euro 2008. And like all big game players, he saved his best performance for the final, against Germany. He never stopped running all game long, helping his team at both ends of the pitch. At the final whistle, Spain were the new European Champions and that was just the start...

11 JULY 2010,
NETHERLANDS 0–1 SPAIN

At the 2010 World Cup in South Africa, Sergio and his Barcelona rivals Carles Puyol and Gerard Piqué only conceded two goals over the entire tournament. And after a hard-fought final against the Netherlands, Spain were crowned the new World Champions. Sergio was also named in the World Cup Dream Team.

24 MAY 2014,
REAL MADRID 4–1 ATLÉTICO MADRID

This was Sergio's first Champions League Final, but he didn't let that faze him. With seconds to go, Real Madrid were losing 1–0 to their local rivals, Atlético. Sergio had scored two goals in the semi-final against Bayern Munich, and he scored again in the final to rescue his team. As the cross came in, he rose highest to head the ball down into the bottom corner. 1–1! Real Madrid went on to win 4–1 in extra time, but it was all thanks to Sergio.

21 JUNE 2016, REAL MADRID 1–1
ATLÉTICO MADRID (5–3 ON PENS)

Another Champions League final against Atlético, another goal from Sergio. This time, he gave Real Madrid the lead, and with his foot rather than his head. When the match then went to penalties, Sergio stepped up and coolly scored their fourth spot-kick, before Cristiano Ronaldo blasted home the winner.

PLAY LIKE YOUR HEROES

THE SERGIO RAMOS HERO HEADER

STEP 1: When your team wins a corner-kick, race forward from defence. You might not be the tallest player on the pitch, but you're a big game winner!

STEP 2: Once you reach the edge of the opposition box, slow down to have a quick chat with your teammates and discuss the tactics. After all, you need to make sure that you're making different runs into the danger zone!

STEP 3: While you wait for the cross to come in, bounce up and down on your toes. You need to be ready to react fast.

STEP 4: Just as your team's corner taker strikes the ball, go, go, go! Make your move from the back post to the front post, and escape from your marker.

STEP 5: As you move, make sure that you watch the flight of the ball, all the way onto your head...

STEP 6: BANG! As you jump up, flick your head round to power the ball towards the... GOAL!

TEST YOUR KNOWLEDGE

QUESTIONS

1. Which football tournament did little Sergio watch Spain win in 1992?

2. What was the name of the boy that Sergio had to pretend to be when he first joined Camas Juniors?

3. Which Spanish club scouted Sergio when he was ten years old?

4. How old was Sergio when he made his La Liga debut and in what position did he play?

5. Which manager first called Sergio up to the Spain national team?

6. How much money did Real Madrid pay to sign Sergio in 2005?

7. Who was the manager of Spain when Sergio and co won the World Cup in 2010?

8. What happened to Sergio in the 2012 Champions League semi-final?

9. Who did Sergio replace as Real Madrid captain in 2015?

10. How many World Cups has Sergio played at and how many goals has he scored?

11. How many goals has Sergio scored in Champions League finals, excluding penalties?

Answers below. . . No cheating!

1. *The Olympics* 2. *Pepito* 3. *Sevilla, his local team* 4. *17 years old and right-back* 5. *Luis Aragonés* 6. *€27 million* 7. *Vicente del Bosque, or 'El Mister.'* 8. *He missed a penalty in the shoot-out against Bayern Munich, which Real Madrid lost* 9. *Iker Casillas* 10. *Four World Cups (2006, 2010, 2014, 2018) but zero goals!* 11. *Two (one in 2014, one in 2016), plus a penalty in the 2016 shoot-out!*

6.

7.

8.

9.

10.

11.

DE GEA

TABLE OF CONTENTS

CHAPTER 1

THE GREAT WALL

13 January 2019, Wembley Stadium

As they waited in the tunnel, many of the Manchester United players were too excited to stand still. Star striker Marcus Rashford jumped up and down, midfield general Ander Herrera shook out his arms and legs, and captain Ashley Young clapped and cheered.

'This is it, lads – let's get stuck in straight away!'

David, however, stayed as calm and composed as ever. What was there to worry about? If his teammates needed him, United's Number One keeper would be there to save the day.

It had been a bad start to the Premier League

season, both for David and his football club. However, things were starting to look a lot brighter. Under new manager Ole Gunnar Solskjær, United had won six games out of six. They had their confidence back, but this would be their first big test – Tottenham away.

For David, that meant the tough task of stopping Harry Kane, one of the sharpest shooters in the world. Kane wasn't Tottenham's only amazing attacker either – they also had Son Heung-min, and Dele Alli, and Christian Eriksen.

David, however, was determined. Despite a difficult 2018 World Cup, he was still one of the greatest goalkeepers in the world. It was time to prove it. At his best, he was absolutely unbeatable!

'And I'm back to my best now,' he told himself confidently, as the match kicked off.

In the first half, David didn't have very much to do. Instead, United were up at the other end of the pitch, attacking. Paul Pogba played a brilliant pass to Rashford and he scored past Hugo Lloris. *1–0!*

'Yes!' David yelled, throwing his arms up in the air.

Right, time to really focus. He was about to become a very busy keeper. United were winning at Wembley, and it was David's job to keep it that way.

Kane fired a shot towards the far corner, but he stretched out his long right leg. SAVE!

David loved showing off his fantastic footwork. It was something that he had worked hard on with his first United goalkeeping coach, Eric Steele. Now, it was his superpower, his most dangerous weapon – but by no means his only weapon. When Alli steered a header towards the bottom corner, he dived down and stretched out his long arms just in time. SAVE!

'Who was marking him?' David wondered, but he didn't say it out loud – he wasn't a shouter like his United hero, Peter Schmeichel. Instead, he just got up and prepared himself for his next performance...

Alli burst through the United defence, but David stood up big and tall to block the shot. SAVE!

The Tottenham players couldn't believe it. Was there an invisible wall in front of the goal? No, it was just David, United's Great Wall.

Tottenham had chance after chance, but David

made save after save.

Toby Alderweireld kicked the ball early on the volley, but David stretched out his long left leg. SAVE!

Kane's fierce free kick was curling in, but David flew through the air like superman. SAVE!

Not only did David keep the ball out, he managed to catch the ball too! 'Nice one!' the United centre-back Phil Jones said, giving his great goalkeeper a hug.

Tottenham weren't giving up yet, though. Alli got the ball in the penalty area again – would he be third time lucky? No, there was just no way past David. ANOTHER SAVE!

David never let his focus slip, not even for a second. Kane took another shot, but David stretched out his long right leg so far that he did the splits! SAVE!

'Are you okay?' Phil asked him, looking worried. 'That looked painful!'

David nodded calmly. He was fine – no big deal! In the last minute of the game, Érik Lamela swung a corner into the box, and David rushed out bravely to punch the ball downfield. It was the perfect way to end a perfect display.

As soon as the final whistle blew, David was surrounded by his thankful teammates.

'What a hero!' Ashley screamed in his face.

'We could have played another ninety minutes and they still wouldn't have scored!' Ander added.

'How many saves did you make?' Phil asked. 'I lost count ages ago!'

There were lots more happy hugs to come; with Ole, his manager; with Emilio Alvarez, his goalkeeping coach; and with his friend and teammate, Juan Mata.

Juan looked shocked, as if he'd just watched a magic show. 'I've never seen anything like it!' he said, with a huge smile on his face.

The United fans felt the same way. They clapped and clapped for their super keeper, singing his song over and over again:

He's big, he's brave, he's Spanish Dave,
He makes big saves, he never shaves,
He's flying through the air,

Come and have a shot if you dare!

Amongst those clapping along was Sir Alex
Ferguson, the old Manchester United manager
who had first brought him to England from Atlético
Madrid. Even during his early 'Dodgy Keeper!' days,
Sir Alex had been sure that David would one day go
on to become one of the best in the world.

José de Gea had always believed in his son too.
David had suffered setbacks along the way, but he
had bounced back every time. That resilience was
a crucial part of being a great goalkeeper. José knew
that from experience. Yes, he was a very, very proud
dad indeed.

CHAPTER 2

LIKE FATHER, LIKE SON

'Go on, son, take your best shot!' José called out, clapping his goalkeeper gloves together. 'I'm ready!'

Football was the De Gea family's favourite sport – so much so that José had even set up a mini-goal in their living room.

'It's not for me,' he promised his wife, Marivi. 'It's for David! I just want to give him the best possible start in life.'

It certainly seemed to be working. David fixed his eyes on the ball in front of him, with a look of real concentration on his little face. He was ready too – ready to score a great goal against his dad. As he ran forward, he pulled back his leg and kicked with all his might. *BANG!*

'What a shot!' José shouted out proudly as the ball flew towards him. It was a clean strike, with plenty of power. At the age of three, David already had a real rocket of a right foot. 'Like father like son,' José thought to himself happily. Of course, he let the ball roll under his diving body and into the back of the net.

'Noooooooooooooo!' José pretended to cry, slapping the carpet.

'GOOOOOOOOOOOOOOOAAAAAAAAAAAAAAAAAA AALLLLLLLLLLLLLLLLLL!' David screamed, running around the living room in circles, before jumping up and down on the sofa.

'Right – what next?' José asked, when his son had finally calmed down again. 'Do you want to take a few more shots?'

David shook his head.

'Okay, have you had enough for today?'

David shook his head again.

'My turn!' he said with a big smile.

His dad smiled too. 'What, you want to go in goal, eh? Like father, like son!'

José had been a professional keeper for Elche and Getafe, two football clubs who played in Spain's lower leagues. He had higher hopes for his son, however – David was going to play for the De Gea family's favourite football team, Atlético Madrid.

David had been born in Spain's capital city, but soon afterwards, the family moved away to a nearby town called Illescas. Still, he had already learned to cheer 'Atleti!' whenever he saw the red and white stripes on TV.

'Here you go,' José said, taking off his gloves and giving them to his son, but there was just one problem. When David put them on, they looked more like oven gloves than goalkeeper gloves on his tiny hands! No, he wouldn't be able to save anything with those on.

'Ha ha, maybe those will fit you in a few years!' José laughed. 'But for now...'

He rushed out of the room and returned with something hidden behind his back.

'...what do you think of these?'

David's eyes lit up – his own brand-new pair of kids' gloves! They were still a little big for him, but it was much better than wearing his dad's oven gloves.

'Right, are you ready?' José asked, placing the mini-ball on the mini-penalty spot.

David clapped his new gloves together, copying his dad exactly. 'GO!'

As the ball flew towards him, he watched it carefully, stretched out his right hand and...

'What a save!' his dad shouted out proudly. Whether he was scoring goals or stopping goals, David was a football natural.

'Like father, like son,' José thought to himself happily.

CHAPTER 3

FUTSAL STAR

Scoring goals or stopping goals? That was David's big decision. It was a really difficult choice to make because he was brilliant at both.

At his first school, *Colegio Castilla*, David chose to focus on scoring. Being the star striker was just more fun, especially when he was playing with his friends. Every day, he raced through the school gates, threw his bag down, and started the morning match.

'Let's go, we haven't got long before the bell!'

If David wasn't in class, he was almost always outside playing sport. He loved basketball and tennis too, but football was his favourite thing to do. Sometimes, they did keepy-uppies or headers and volleys in the playground, and other times, they played futsal – five-a-side indoor football – in the sports hall.

It didn't take the school team coach, José María Cruz, long to notice David's talent. In the passing and shooting drills, most of the youngsters just tried to kick the ball as hard as they possibly could. Their wild shots went everywhere, but usually high and wide.

'Don't forget to aim for the target!' Cruz got bored of telling them.

But there was one tall, skinny boy who already had the right idea. When the goal was there in front of him, he kept his cool and placed his shot right in the bottom corner.

'Fantastic finish! What's your name?' Cruz asked the blond-haired boy.

'David,' he replied.

'Well, David, congratulations! You're going to be our new striker.'

'Great!' he thought to himself. As much as David enjoyed playing in goal at home with his dad, it seemed like strikers got a lot more glory. Take his favourite team, Atleti, for example. Their keeper, José

Francisco Molina, was so good that he also played in goal for the Spanish national team, but he was still nowhere near as famous as the club's new Number 9, Christian Vieri.

The message of that story? Everyone loves the guy who gets the goals! So, like most six-year-olds, David decided that he wanted to be Vieri, rather than Molina. In no time at all, he was the top scorer for the *Colegio Castilla* futsal team.

Dani slid the ball through to him and... *GOAL!*

David played a one-two with Juan and... *GOAL!*

Opposition defenders tried to stop David, with a tough tackle or a big push, but... *GOAL!*

'I reckon we could blindfold you, and you'd still score every time!' Cruz joked.

David wasn't just a fantastic finisher, though. As he grew older, he kept improving as an all-round footballer. He had the style of futsal to thank for that. The pitch was much smaller, and the ball was much heavier, so a defender couldn't just hoof it all the way up the field to the striker! No, futsal was all about touch and technique. To be a top player, you had to be able to pass and dribble your way out of small spaces, even as a striker.

'Check this out!' David announced to his teammates. He was about to try out a cool new trick in training. Carlos and Juan had boxed him in by the corner flag, but with a stepover, then a drag-back and then a backheel, he escaped with the ball. *GOAL!*

'Skillz!' Dani clapped and cheered.

David was well on his way to becoming a top futsal player, and that made José a very, very proud dad indeed. He was there at every match, cheering his son on. Although he was a striker at the moment, José still hoped that David might one day carry on the family tradition.

'Did you know that Pepe Reina started out as an attacker, just like you?' José told his son as they drove home from a game one day. He was trying to sound as casual as possible, but that name had certainly grabbed David's attention.

'Really?' he replied excitedly. Reina had just become Barcelona's new star goalkeeper.

'Yes, the best goalkeepers are always brilliant all-round footballers. You have to have skilful feet, as well as safe hands!'

'Cool, thanks, Dad!'

Marivi was a very proud mum too, but sometimes she worried that David was spending too much time running around with a ball at his feet, and not enough time sitting down doing his homework.

'Education is important!' she warned him again and again. 'If you don't study hard, you'll regret it one day.'

Just because his dad had become a professional footballer, that didn't mean that David would become one too. These things didn't just run in the family. He would need to have amazing talent, the right attitude, and good fortune as well. Marivi wanted her son to have a Plan B, just in case.

'How is David doing?' she often called up to ask his teachers. 'Is he paying attention in class? Does he seem tired? That boy plays so much sport, but school must come first.'

'Don't worry,' they always reassured her. 'David is doing just fine!'

At *Colegio Castilla*, David continued to be a star

CHAPTER 4

THE POPLAR AND THE GREAT DANE

futsal striker. Outside of school, however, he decided to follow in his father's footsteps instead.

'Are you sure?' José asked him. The last thing he wanted to do was force his son to play a position that he hated.

But David just nodded. He was happy because putting on the goalkeeper gloves felt so familiar to him. It was like returning home, and it made sense for so many reasons:

1) He was tall for his age,
2) He was always calm,
3) He had really good reflexes for saving shots,
4) When he dived, he could fly through the air

like superman,

And most importantly of all,

5) His dad was a goalkeeper too!

José was always there to give David lessons, whenever he wanted. There was nothing he liked more than talking about football. Every day was a school day in the De Gea house.

'Son, have I ever told you about "The Poplar"?' José asked David one afternoon.

He looked confused. 'No, what's that?'

'Well, a poplar is a tree, but it was also what they used to call José Ángel Iribar, my favourite goalkeeper of all time.'

'Why did they call him that?'

'Because when he came out to catch the ball, he jumped up tall and straight, just like a tree.'

'Did "The Poplar" play for Spain?' David asked.

'Yes, lots of times! He even played at the World Cup in 1966.'

'Cool! And did he play for Atleti too?'

'No, sadly not. He's from the Basque country, and

so he chose to spend his whole career at Athletic Bilbao.'

'But why do you like him so much, Dad? What was so special about him?'

'I think it's easier if I just show you instead,' José said, searching for footage on the Internet. 'A-ha, found it! Here, let's watch this.'

Some of the video footage was so old that it was in black and white! But David didn't mind that; for him, watching 'The Poplar' in goal was like watching the most exciting action movie ever.

Iribar throwing himself down bravely at the feet of a striker,

Iribar jumping high to catch a cross.

'Hey, he's not even wearing gloves in that one!' David pointed out to his dad.

Iribar punching the ball out of the box,

Iribar tipping a free kick over the crossbar.

David's eyes stayed fixed on the computer screen, even after the video had ended.

'So, what did you think?' José asked eventually.

'I think he's... AMAZING!' David replied, his

voice full of awe.

'Correct answer!' his dad laughed. 'Did you notice how quickly he moved across his goal? Incredible! They should have called him "The Panther", not "The Poplar"! But do you know what he was best at?'

'Catching?'

José shook his head.

'Kicking?'

José shook his head again.

'Concentrating! Being a goalkeeper can be a boring job at times. If your team is off attacking at the other end of the pitch, you don't have much to do. Some keepers switch off and lose their focus, but not Iribar. Never! "The Poplar" was always alert, always ready to save the day.'

In Iribar, David had his second goalkeeping hero (his first being his dad, of course!), and by the age of nine, he had his third.

David and José watched lots and lots of football together on TV – all the Atleti games, but also lots of Champions League matches. For a young boy, it was so exciting to see so many excellent teams from all over Europe: Juventus from Italy, Dynamo Kyiv from Ukraine, Bayern Munich from Germany, and, best of all, Manchester United from England.

They were David's new favourite team. Sir Alex Ferguson's team had it all –

Ole Gunnar Solskjær's shooting,

Teddy Sheringham's heading,

Ryan Giggs's dribbling,

David Beckham's crossing,

Paul Scholes's passing,

Roy Keane's tackling,

and, best of all,

Peter Schmeichel's shotstopping.

David had never seen a goalkeeper like Schmeichel before. His nickname was 'The Great Dane', partly because he was from Denmark, but also partly because he was big and loved to bark, just like the dog.

'If I was a United defender, I'd be terrified of him!' José joked.

But there was a lot more to Schmeichel than just his shouting. He could make all kinds of super saves and when he jumped up in front of a striker, he pretty much blocked the whole goal!

It was 26 May 1999: Manchester United vs Bayern Munich at the Nou Camp in Barcelona. That Champions League Final was a night that David would never forget. It started with Schmeichel walking out on to the pitch as United captain, wearing his bright green goalkeeper shirt.

'Come on, Schmeichel!' David cheered, watching the game on TV in Spain.

And it ended with Solskjær scoring the winning goal in the very last minute of the match.

'Manchester! Manchester!' David shouted at the TV screen.

It hadn't been a busy night for 'The Great Dane', but he had still made two top saves to keep United in the game. Sheringham and Solskjær got the glory, but Schmeichel was the hero in David's eyes.

A few weeks later at school, the teacher asked the class to write down their plans for the future. David's answer was short and sweet:

'I want to be like Peter Schmeichel.'

Yes, David dreamed of playing in goal for Manchester United, and winning the Champions League.

CHAPTER 5

CASARRUBUELOS

But how was David going to make his Manchester United dream come true? By working hard and listening to his coaches, that's how. Thankfully, he had two excellent people helping him.

First, there was his dad. José didn't just watch all of David's matches; he watched most of his training sessions too. Even in the freezing winter, with the rain lashing down on his umbrella, José was there, watching carefully. He was always honest with his son. If David played a blinder, he told him so. And if he had a stinker, he still told him so.

'Don't worry, there's always next week to put things right,' José liked to say. 'Learning from your mistakes is an important part of becoming a great goalkeeper.'

And then there was David's coach at Casarrubuelos, Juan Luis Martín. Casarrubuelos were a local youth club who were linked with David's favourite football team, Atlético Madrid. He even got to wear their badge proudly on his goalkeeper shirt.

'One day, you're going to be Atleti's Number One!' Martín wisely predicted.

The Casarrubuelos coach could see straight away that David had a very special talent. He was tall but also very agile, and he didn't mind diving across his goal, even on hard, dry pitches. In fact, he seemed to love it. And not only was he safe with his hands, but he was also skilful with his feet.

Yes, David was a very promising player indeed, but he needed to keep challenging himself in order to reach the top level. So each week, Martín came up with new tests for his young goalkeeper to complete.

'Right, you've got to catch thirty crosses in a row,' he said.

Easy! David had watched 'The Poplar' a million

times, after all.

'Okay, I want to see you make ten saves to your left, then ten to your right.'

Easy! Thanks to José's coaching, he was strong on both sides.

David passed every test with flying colours – saving penalties, saving free kicks, saving one-on-ones, throwing, kicking, concentrating...

In the end, Martín could only smile and accept defeat. 'Fine, I guess you're just a natural, then!'

David's teammates definitely agreed. They loved having him there between the posts. The defenders didn't have to worry so much about making mistakes when they had the best goalkeeper in the league behind them.

The opposition striker was through on goal, with just David to beat... *BLOCK!*

A shot flew like an arrow towards the top corner of David's goal... *SAVE!*

The rebound fell to the striker, but David bounced back up... *DOUBLE SAVE!*

'Sorry!' his defenders panted as they chased back

into position, but David never shouted at them like Schmeichel would have done. He preferred to stay calm and composed. Besides, he was just doing his job, after all.

'Please don't ever leave us,' Javier the centre-back begged. 'We'd fall apart without you!'

David enjoyed being the Casarrubuelos hero, but he had his heart set on bigger things: Atleti, Manchester United, Spain...

As he cheered his country on at the 2002 World Cup, David tried to imagine what it would feel like to be Iker Casillas. But that was impossible! At the age of only twenty-one, Casillas was already the Number One goalkeeper for Real Madrid *and* Spain.

'You can be that good,' José told his son confidently, 'if not even better.'

Really? David could see from his dad's face that he meant it. As good as Casillas? He was incredible, a super-keeper!

No, David couldn't think like that. He had to be confident and believe in himself. Otherwise, how would he ever go on and achieve his dreams?

'I can be that good,' he told his reflection in the mirror.

In his mind, David pictured a future Madrid Derby. The Vicente Calderón Stadium was like a bubbling cauldron of noise as the two teams walked out onto the pitch and took up their positions. In goal for Real, Iker Casillas. And in goal for Atleti... David de Gea!

CHAPTER 6

CATCHING ATLETI'S ATTENTION

If David kept saving the day for Casarrubuelos, surely an Atleti scout would eventually notice and sign him up. That was the plan, but what if that never happened?

'Just be patient,' José reassured him. 'You're twelve, not twenty-one!'

David tried to follow his dad's advice as usual, but patience wasn't easy. He had done his research on the Internet: Casillas had joined the Real Madrid youth academy at the age of nine, and he had been called up to the senior squad at the age of sixteen. For David, that was only four years away!

As he warmed up before each match, he looked around the edge of the pitch, searching for unfamiliar faces in the crowd, trying to identify a possible football scout. But who could it be? The old man wearing a hat? The woman under the umbrella? The young man walking his dog?

One person who did know the answer to that question was Martín, the Casarrubuelos coach. He was always on the lookout for scouts, just like David. He really didn't want to lose his star keeper, but at the same time, he didn't want to hold him back from reaching his full potential. David had the talent to go on and play for the Atleti first team; he was sure of it.

So, when one day an Atlético youth coach asked him if he had any good young goalkeepers, Martín mentioned David's name straight away.

'You're in luck, Emilio. I've got just the kid you're looking for!'

Martín talked the coach through David's many talents – the super saves, the brave blocks, the long throws, the accurate kicks.

'Why don't you come and watch him play next week? Trust me, you'll like him! The boy's dad will be there, and you can have a chat with him.

Remember José de Gea? He used to play in goal for Getafe in the eighties.'

'Yeah, that name rings a bell,' Emilio García replied. 'Thanks Juan, we'll check this kid out.'

Weeks passed, however, and there was no sign of the Atleti youth coach. Martín hadn't heard from him, and neither had David and José. Had García simply found a better young keeper somewhere else? Or was he just taking a very long time?

'Don't worry, I'll give him a call and find out what's going on,' Martín reassured his young keeper.

Was there anything more that the Casarrubuelos coach could do to help David? After a lot of thought, he came up with a clever plan.

'Emilio, are you still looking for a young keeper?' Martín asked on the phone.

'Yes, sorry, I've just been so busy recently,' Emilio García explained.

'No problem, but I just thought I'd let you know that Rayo Vallecano are ready to make David an offer. So, if you're interested, you need to come down here quick.'

Yes, it was a lie, but it was only a little white lie! What harm could it possibly do?

There were a few seconds of silence as García decided what to do next. 'Okay Juan, I'm sending someone to watch your game this weekend.'

'Great, I'll let the boy's family know,' Martín said, smiling to himself. His clever plan had worked perfectly!

García didn't just send any old scout to watch David play; he sent Diego Díaz Garrido, a goalkeeper who had played over sixty games for Atlético Madrid.

David recognised him as soon as he arrived at the Casarrubuelos ground. *GULP!* This was it, the big opportunity. Now the pressure was really on.

'Try not to think about it,' José told him before kick-off. 'Just go out there and play your normal game. Show him what you can do!'

David nodded and clapped his gloves together, just like his dad used to do.

Fortunately, he didn't have to wait long to be called into action. First, he made a good save to tip a shot past the post, and then he came out to catch the corner kick.

'Great work, David!' Martín cheered on the sidelines. He took a quick glance over at the Atlético scout. Surely, he was impressed?

He was. Diego had seen lots of young keepers who were good at some things, and not so good at other things. They all had weaknesses – but not this kid at Casarrubuelos.

David had the height, the reflexes, the bravery, the composure, *and* the understanding of the game. He was brilliant at saving, catching, throwing *and* kicking.

Yes, this David de Gea was the real deal, the complete package. There was no question about it. The opposition strikers had absolutely no chance of scoring past him.

As soon as the referee blew the half-time whistle, Diego was on the phone to García.

'So, what do you think?' the Atleti youth coach asked.

His reply was short and simple. 'Sign him straight away.'

CHAPTER 7

LIFE AT *LA CANTERA*

When he heard the news, David jumped for joy. His lifelong wish was about to come true. The De Gea family's favourite football team, Atlético Madrid, wanted to sign him.

'I did it, Dad!' David screamed. 'I did it!'

José wiped away his tears of pride and laughed heartily. 'My son, the Atleti star!'

David wasn't there yet, though. He still had a long way to go before his Madrid Derby dream became a reality, before he was competing against Casillas.

That was clear as soon as he arrived at *La Cantera*, the home of the club's youth academy. David just sat there staring out of the car window, with his mouth wide open. Wow, what a beautiful sight! There were hundreds of happy kids practising their football skills on perfect green pitches, with Spanish hills rising up in the distance.

As David watched them all warming up, suddenly the nerves set in. Atlético was going to be a big step-up from Casarrubuelos. What if he wasn't good enough? What if he made a total fool of himself? What if he couldn't save any of the strikers' shots?

With each doubt that entered his head, David's panic grew. Thankfully, his mum was there by his side to calm him down.

'Go on, you've got nothing to fear,' Marivi told him gently. 'Just enjoy yourself!'

David nodded, opened the car door and walked bravely into *La Cantera*.

García was there to welcome him and introduce him to the other Atlético Under-14 players. As he did, David just stood there, smiling shyly at all the unfamiliar faces. Being the new kid was rubbish!

One thing that David noticed straight away was the size of his teammates. He was one of the tallest, but he was also the skinniest. Some of the big boys could have snapped him like a little twig. And, judging by the evil glares, the other goalkeeper wanted to do just that!

GULP! It was a mighty relief when the training session started. After a bit of catching practice, David was put in goal for a shooting drill.

'Right, time to shine,' he muttered to himself.

He took a long, deep breath and danced from foot to foot. He was ready to fly through the sky like Superman. He was going to do everything possible to keep this ball out of the net. He needed to make an incredible first impression.

The striker played a one-two and ran on to the return pass. As he pulled his leg back to shoot, David searched for clues.

Which foot would he use? Right.

Which side of the goal would the striker aim for? He was looking low to David's left.

Would he go for power or accuracy? Unfortunately, David wouldn't really know that until the very last second.

BANG! The striker curled the ball towards

the bottom corner. David sprang across his goal, stretching out his long left arm as far as it would go… *SAVE!*

'Nice one, keeper!' his new coach clapped and cheered.

David was delighted but he didn't show any emotion. He just picked himself up off the grass and prepared to save the next shot too.

'So, how did it go?' his mum asked on the long journey back to Illescas.

David shrugged. 'Okay, thanks.'

Marivi was used to her son's short replies; he was a teenager now. 'And?' she added.

'The coach says I'll be starting in goal for the match on Sunday.'

'That's my boy!' she cried out. 'Congratulations, I knew you could do it!'

It turned out that playing for Atleti was exactly the challenge that David needed. He thrived under the pressure, making supersave after supersave against the best young strikers in Spain.

'Man, how did we cope before you came along?'

the left-back Álvaro Domínguez wondered.

David smiled and shrugged. What could he say? First Casarrubuelos and now Atleti; he just loved being the hero!

'What did I tell you?' his dad said with a smirk. 'My son, the Atleti star!'

Even though *La Cantera* was a long way from Illescas, José hardly missed a minute of David's performances. He didn't just watch all of his son's matches; he watched most of his training sessions too. Even during the freezing winter, with the rain lashing down on his umbrella, José was there, watching carefully.

And even though Atlético had some of the top goalkeeper trainers in the country, David still always listened to his dad's advice. José had been his first coach and he would always be his most important. So he would always reply: 'Yes, Dad!' or 'Thanks, Dad!'

But just when David felt like he had conquered *La Cantera*, a new challenge came his way. Suddenly, he wasn't the only talented young keeper at Atleti.

Joel Robles was the same age as David, and even taller. He was also already a Spanish Under-16 international.

'You need to show this new guy who's boss!' Domínguez told him, but that wasn't David's style. He wasn't a shouter like Schmeichel. He would let his saves do the talking.

Off the pitch, David and Joel became good friends. On the pitch, however, they became fierce rivals, fighting to be Atleti's future Number One. The battle helped to bring out the best in both of them.

'That spot is *mine!*' David told himself after pulling off yet another wondersave.

No, David wasn't the loudest, but he was the most determined. Anything Joel could do, he could do too. Soon, David was off on an international adventure of his own.

CHAPTER 8

2007: A SPECIAL SPANISH SUMMER

'Come on, we can win this!' David told his
Spanish teammates confidently as they set off for
Belgium to play in the UEFA European Under-17
Championship.

He couldn't wait to represent his country in a
proper, major tournament. What a proud moment it
would be! So far, everything was going according to
his football dreams. First the Spain Under-15s, and
now the Under-17s. He was following in the glove-
prints of his goalkeeper heroes like José 'The Poplar'
Iribar and Iker Casillas.

Viva España!

After twenty-four years of disappointment, at last

the future of the Spanish national team looked bright again. Now, they had a senior squad full of superstars like Xavi, Casillas, Andrés Iniesta and David Villa. '*La Roja*' could beat anyone, and so could their Under-17s.

The core of Spain's youth team was incredible: Barcelona's Bojan in attack, Arsenal's Fran Mérida in midfield, Real Madrid's Nacho in defence and, of course, David in goal! He was wearing Number 13, rather than Number 1, but there was no doubt that he was the first-choice stopper.

'Yes, we've got the talent,' their coach Juan Santisteban told them, 'but have we got the winning mentality? If we're not focused, we'll fail!'

David was always focused. That was one of the many things that made him such a clever keeper. Neither France nor Germany could score past him.

'Yes, that's two clean sheets already!' David cheered, high-fiving Nacho. To them, they were almost as important as goals.

Spain were through to the semi-finals! Next up were Belgium and their deadly attacking duo,

Christian Benteke and Eden Hazard. David made
some super saves but there was nothing he could do
when Hazard's shot deflected off Spain's defender,
David Rochela.

'Noooo!' David's heart sank. He really hated letting
in goals.

But luckily, Bojan equalised and, after extra time,
the semi-final went to penalties. As a goalkeeper,
this was David's time to shine. He could become a
national hero!

As the first Belgian player placed the ball down on
the spot, David took a long, deep breath and threw
his long arms out, high and wide. He was ready to fly
through the sky like Superman.

But De Pauw scored,
and so did Spruyt,
and so did Zevne,
and so did Hazard...

Aquino didn't score, but he blazed over the bar.
After seven penalties each, David still hadn't made a
single save.

'Come on!' he told himself. 'Stop this next one,

and we're in the final!'

He looked up and saw his teammates on the
halfway line, cheering him on. They were counting
on him.

Belgium's captain Dimitri Daeseleire stepped up
and… SAVE!

David got back to his feet and punched the air
with both fists. He had done it – he was Spain's spot-
kick hero! Seconds later, he was at the bottom of a
big pile of grateful players.

'Thanks, what a save!'

'You're a legend!'

Viva España!

In the UEFA European Under-17 Championship
Final, it was Spain vs England. Could David and co.
keep a third clean sheet?

When Bojan scored early in the second half, David
threw his arms up in the air. However, he didn't let
his focus slip. The match was still far from over.

With half an hour to go, England fired a fizzing
free kick towards the bottom corner. The Spain
defenders turned, fearing the worst, but David dived

down and stretched out his long left arm as far as it would go... *SAVE!*

David was delighted but he didn't show it. He just pulled up his socks and got ready for the corner-kick.

When the referee blew the final whistle, the Spain players ran towards each other and bounced up and down together. David was one of the last to join the happy huddle. On the sideline, their coaches were doing the same thing.

What an achievement – Spain were the Champions of Europe! And that meant their international adventure was only just beginning. In August, David and his teammates travelled to South Korea to challenge for the FIFA Under-17 World Cup trophy.

'Right, let's keep this run going!' Santisteban urged his players and they listened.

Spain 4 Honduras 2

Spain 2 Syria 1

Spain 1 Argentina 1

David was disappointed that he hadn't kept any clean sheets yet, but there was still time for that.

Spain were through to the next round.

Against North Korea, David didn't have much to do, but he never let his focus slip.

'Concentrate!' he kept telling himself. 'At some point, your team will need you.'

David was right. A shot deflected off a Spanish defender and changed direction completely. Suddenly, the ball was curling into the bottom corner... no, SAVE!

What a stop! David certainly deserved his first clean sheet of the tournament. 'Quarter-finals, here we come!' he cheered at the final whistle.

Spain had beaten France 2–0 at the Euros, but it was a much more competitive match at the World Cup. After 120 minutes, the score was still 1–1. Time for penalties! As a goalkeeper, it was David's time to shine once more.

'We believe in you!' Bojan said, giving him a big hug. 'We need you to be our spot-kick hero again!'

But Sakho scored,

and so did Le Tallec. *2–2!*

'I should have got my glove to that one!' David

moaned. But there was no time for self-criticism, he had to keep focus and keep believing in himself. He clapped his gloves together and prepared for the next penalty. 'All I have to do is make one save, and we're in the semi-finals!'

Thibault Bourgeois stepped up and... SAVE!

'Yes!' David roared like a lion.

Thanks to their super-keeper, Spain now had the advantage.

Bojan scored,

and so did Fran,

and so did Dani Aquino. They were the winners!

'Next time, can we just win in normal time please?' David teased his relieved teammates.

Spain didn't beat Ghana in ninety minutes, but they did beat them in 120. Just when another penalty shoot-out was looming, Bojan scored the winning goal. *Phew!*

David's dream had come true. He was about to play in a World Cup Final – Spain vs Nigeria.

As the two teams walked out onto the pitch, it really felt like a final. The stadium was filled with over 36,000 fans. That meant four times more noise than in the semis!

During the national anthems, David soaked up the amazing atmosphere around him. But as soon as the music stopped, he was fully focused on winning another trophy. Spain were the favourites, but that meant nothing now.

'Let's do this!' David cheered.

But as hard as they tried, neither team could score.

First, Spain had a shot cleared off the line.

'Ohhhhhhhh!' David groaned with his hands on his head.

Then, Nigeria's left winger cut inside and went for goal. It was a powerful strike, but not powerful enough to get past David. He sprang up and tipped the ball over the bar.

'Thanks, superman!' Nacho said, patting him on the back.

The game was goalless after 90 minutes, and it was still goalless after 120 minutes too. It was time for one last penalty shoot-out.

David was desperate to be Spain's spot-kick hero in

the World Cup final. Sadly, however, it wasn't to be this time.

Nigeria scored three penalties out of three, while Spain didn't score a single one. 3–0! It was all over in a flash and Nigeria's keeper, Dele Ajiboye, was the spot-kick hero. David's World Cup dream had been destroyed.

'Hey, there was nothing more you could have done,' Santisteban comforted his keeper. 'You were the best goalie in the whole tournament. This is just the start for you!'

David returned home with mixed feelings. It was very disappointing not to win the World Cup, but he was pleased with his performances. He had made a real name for himself during that special Spanish summer. What next?

CHAPTER 9

OUT ON LOAN OR TRAIN ALONE?

When he arrived back at Atlético, David still had a keeper battle to win. Yes, he was improving with every game, but so was Joel. David couldn't just sit back and relax after his achievements with Spain. If he wanted to become an Atleti star one day, he had to keep fighting.

Just like at the Under-17 World Cup, David rose to every challenge that faced him. He stayed fully focused and he didn't put a foot, or glove, wrong. With every super save and brave block, he was proving Diego right; he *was* the complete package, the real deal.

Ultimately, there could only be one winner. As the 2008–09 season loomed, the club made their crucial decision: Joel would play for Atlético Madrid C, and David would play for... Atlético Madrid B!

David had won the battle, and he had his first professional contract to prove it. He would be staying at his favourite football team until at least 2011.

'By then, I'll be the Number One!' he thought to himself.

One challenge completed – on to the next! This was going to be a big step-up for David, maybe even bigger than when he moved from Casarrubuelos to *La Cantera*.

Atlético B played in *Segunda División B*, the third level of the Spanish football league. For the first time, David wouldn't just be playing against his own age group. He was still only eighteen, but now he would be facing strikers who were twenty-five, or thirty, or maybe even thirty-five. Thirty-five? That was nearly twice his age!

'I know you're ready for this,' his dad told him. 'Just remember, get your body behind the ball!'

David wasn't worried. This was just the next step on his road to the top. Besides, Casillas had been even younger when he started his career at Real Madrid C.

Atlético B played thirty-eight league games that season, and David started thirty-five of them. That was more than any other player in the squad. With the team struggling near the bottom of the table, he had plenty of work to do.

David dived down low to keep out a stinging strike. SAVE!

David sprang up and stretched out his long left arm. SAVE!

David stuck out his long right leg to deflect a shot wide. SAVE!

He had already caught the eye of scouts during the Under-17 World Cup, but now he was doing it week-in, week-out for Atlético B. By the summer of 2009, most of Europe's top clubs were scouting him.

Juventus had Gianluigi Buffon for now, but what if he moved on?

Manchester United had Edwin van der Sar for now, but he was nearly at the end of his career. What would happen when he retired?

David would be the ideal replacement for the Dutchman. In Spain, they had even started calling him 'Van der Gea' because their styles were so similar. They were both very tall and skinny, with skilful feet and safe hands. And hadn't David always dreamed of playing for Manchester United?

The plan seemed perfect, but David couldn't leave Spain yet, not before becoming Atleti's Number One.

In Summer 2009, that shirt belonged to Sergio Asenjo, a young keeper who had just signed from Valladolid. And then there was the 'Number 13', Roberto. He was twenty-eight years old, with lots more experience.

'Let the battle begin!' David declared, but the Atlético Madrid Sporting Director disagreed. Jesús García Pitarch wanted his youngest keeper to go out on loan.

'It's the best way for you to keep developing your skills,' Pitarch argued. 'Trust me, you need game-time, not bench-time! I've got two great options for you: stay here in Spain with Numancia or go to England and play for QPR.'

David took some time to talk it through with his

parents. But the more he thought about it, the more he realised that he didn't like either option. What he wanted was to stay at Atlético and prove himself. He was only one year younger than Sergio, and surely, he was good enough to compete?

David wasn't the loudest character at the club, but he could be stubborn when he wanted to be. When he gave Pitarch his answer, the Sporting Director was very angry. 'Fine, well if you won't go out on loan, then you'll have to train alone!'

What? David couldn't believe it, and neither could his parents. It was so unfair! José was all ready to storm into Pitarch's office but Marivi managed to calm him down.

'Give it a few days,' she said. 'Hopefully, he'll change his mind.'

In the end, it worked out brilliantly for David because training alone helped him to stand out even more! One day, Atlético's first team coach, Abel Resino, noticed David doing some catching practice over in the corner of the field. He looked so lonely out there on his own.

'What's going on?' Resino muttered to himself. 'That kid is meant to be Atleti's next great keeper!'

Oh well, if the B team didn't want him, the A team could always use another pair of hands. With two keepers, there was rivalry, but with three, there would be real competition. That could only be a good thing for Atlético.

'Kid, come with me!' Resino shouted across the field.

David nodded eagerly and followed the manager over to where the first team was training. Wow, was this really happening? Yes, it was! David tried to play it as cool as possible, but his heart was thudding like a hammer in his chest.

'Dani, David is joining us today,' Resino called out to one of his coaches. 'I thought our strikers might need some extra shooting practice!'

A few weeks later, Wigan Athletic made a bid to buy David. Their new Spanish manager, Roberto Martínez, was a big fan of the young keeper.

'If you come here, I'll make you a Premier League star!' he promised.

'No thanks!' David replied and this time, Atlético said the same. They didn't want to sell him. Phew! Now he was all set to achieve his lifelong dream: becoming Atleti's Number One.

CHAPTER 10

ON FIRE IN THE FIRST TEAM

Yes, 2009–10 was going to be David's season; he was more determined than ever. However, training with the first team was both exciting and exhausting. This was the big time now. David couldn't switch off for a single second. If he did, the ball was in the back of his net before he even noticed.

'Wake up, David!' the goalkeeping coach shouted. 'You've got to get down quicker!'

It was a steep learning curve for an eighteen-year-old. The Atlético squad was packed with so many fantastic finishers.

When it came to long-range shots, wingers Maxi Rodríguez and Simão Sabrosa could find the top corner with almost every kick. And they could hit the ball so hard! Even when David dived at full stretch, he often couldn't reach out his long arms in time.

'Unlucky, great effort!' the coach encouraged him.

And when it came to close-range shots, Atleti's two South American strikers were the best in the business. The previous season, Uruguayan Diego Forlán had scored the most goals in the entire Spanish league. And Argentinian Sergio Agüero was just as brilliant in the box, if not better. *BANG! GOAL!*

'How am I supposed to stop that?' David asked himself all the time.

He was definitely improving, though, and he was also making friends. He already knew Koke and Domínguez from the youth team, and he discovered that the older players weren't as scary as expected. In fact, they were very friendly.

'Hi, David!' a voice called out in the lunch canteen.

David turned around; it was Agüero. 'Oh, hi Sergio!'

'Call me Kun,' he replied. 'Everyone calls me Kun.'

'My new friend, Kun,' David thought to himself.

'How cool is that?'

Things were about to get even cooler. In
September, Sergio Asenjo went away to play for Spain
at the Under-20 World Cup. That meant that David
was bumped up from third-choice to second-choice
keeper. Now there was only Roberto ahead of him.
David would be there on the bench for Atlético's
next game – Barcelona at the Nou Camp!

'That's wonderful news, son,' José shouted down
the phone. 'Congratulations, we'll be there watching!'

David didn't get to play and Atlético lost, but it
was still an amazing experience for him. When Kun
was substituted, he slumped down in the seat next to
David.

'Don't worry, you'll be out there soon!' the
Argentinian predicted. By the final whistle, Roberto
had let in five goals.

The next week, David watched from the bench as
Atlético drew 2–2 with Almería.

'You should be playing!' his dad argued
passionately.

The week after that, David was on the bench

again, this time in Porto for Atleti's Champions League match. Just when he was sitting comfortably, he was suddenly called into action. After twenty-five minutes, Roberto made a signal to the sidelines. He was injured, and he couldn't carry on.

'David, get ready!' a coach shouted. 'You're coming on!'

What a moment for David to make his Atleti debut! In a flash, he jumped up, took off his tracksuit, and pulled his gloves on. Right, it was his time to shine.

As he jogged into his penalty area, the centre-back Juanito came over. 'Good luck, you're going to be great!'

'Thanks, mate!'

David placed the ball down carefully and sent a long goal kick down the field towards Kun. So far, so good.

At half-time, it was 0–0, and after seventy minutes, it was still 0–0. David was enjoying himself and he was putting on a goalkeeping masterclass.

He pushed a shot past the post. SAVE!

'Well done!' Juanito said, giving David a high-five.

He tipped a free kick over the bar. SAVE!

He came out to clear a cross away. PUNCH!

He bravely blocked a blast from Hulk. SAVE!

Could David keep a clean sheet on his Atleti debut? No, not quite. The ball bounced back to Hulk and he crossed to Radamel Falcao, who backheeled it in. 1–0 to Porto!

'Noooooooo!' David fell to the floor in disappointment. All of his hard work had gone to waste.

He didn't just give up, though. No, he wasn't done yet.

As Falcao headed the ball towards goal, he was sure that he would score... but no, David was there to block it: another SAVE!

'Come on!' David cried out, clapping his gloves together. He could shout like Schmeichel when he needed to.

But from the corner, Falcao hit the post and Rolando tapped in the rebound. 2–0 to Porto!

David was furious at the performance of his side's

defence. What were they doing? He didn't care that he was only eighteen and that it was only his debut; he expected more from his teammates.

At the final whistle, David shook hands with the Porto players and then trudged off the pitch. Resino was waiting for him by the tunnel.

'Kid, you were incredible tonight,' the manager said, patting him on the back. 'You're going to be a superstar!'

Three days later, David made his home debut against Real Zaragoza. He wasn't a sub anymore; he was starting for Atleti at the Vicente Calderón! He had to pinch himself to check that it was real.

David's childhood dream nearly turned into a nightmare, however. After twenty minutes, a Zaragoza midfielder played a through ball into his penalty area. David had to do something, but he made the wrong decision. He raced out and fouled the striker. *Penalty!*

Uh oh, could David make up his mistake? He hoped so. He thought back to his saves for the Spain Under-17s. He could do this.

As Marko Babić ran up, David didn't move. Then at the very last second, he dived down low to his left and... SAVE!

'What a stop!' his teammates ran over to tell him. 'You're a hero!'

David was delighted but he didn't show it. He just got on with the game.

In the second half, Zaragoza did score their second penalty but by then, Atlético had already won the match. At the final whistle, David wasn't ready to leave the field yet. He wanted his big night to go on and on. So, he walked all the way around the pitch, clapping the fans.

Wait, what were they singing? At first, David couldn't believe what he was hearing. The Atleti supporters were chanting his name!

De Gea! De Gea! De Gea!

CHAPTER 11

EL NIÑO WINS THE EUROPA LEAGUE

Despite David's amazing displays, Sergio Asenjo returned from the Under-20 World Cup and went straight back into the Atlético team, replacing David.

'Bring back De Gea!' the fans begged when they lost 3–0 to Osasuna.

There were moans and groans, and plenty of boos. Something had to change. At this point, Atleti were placed seventeenth in the Spanish league, only one point above the relegation zone.

'We finished fourth last season!' people complained.

By October 2009, Atlético had a new manager, Quique Sánchez Flores. And for David, that also meant a new goalkeeping coach.

'Think of this as a fresh start,' Emilio Álvarez announced at the first training session. 'It's time to shine, guys. I want to see what each of you can do.'

Sánchez Flores had asked him to take a look at all three of Atlético's stoppers:

1) Sergio Asenjo, the current Number One,
2) Roberto, the experienced back-up,
And 3) David, the kid, or '*El Niño*' as coaches called him.

'So, what did you think?' the manager asked when they met up in the afternoon.

Emilio had his answer ready. 'The best of the three is *El Niño.*'

Sánchez Flores nodded: 'Then he'll be our keeper.'

David still wore the 'Number 43' shirt, but before long, he was really Atlético's Number One. Even when he made costly errors, they stuck with him.

'These things happen,' Emilio explained, 'especially when you're a young goalie. What matters is how you learn from your mistakes.'

Wasn't that exactly what José had always told him? Emilio firmly believed that David would one day become one of the best keepers around. Just like David's old Casarrubuelos coach Martín, Emilio was always setting crazy new challenges for him to complete.

'Wait, why do I have to wear a blindfold?' David asked. He didn't like not being able to see anything. It was unsettling. 'You're not going to fire balls at me, are you?'

'Don't worry,' the goalkeeping coach replied, 'only from close range! It's to improve your reflexes. Right, are you ready? Go!'

With Emilio, every training session was exciting and different. David never knew what he was going to do next, but whatever it was, it always helped to make him a better keeper.

With David in goal, Atlético leapt back up the league table. Their recovery began when they beat Barcelona. At the Vicente Calderón, Diego and Simão put them 2–0 up after twenty-three minutes. While the fans went wild, their keeper kept calm.

'Stay focused!' David called out to his defenders, clapping his gloves together.

Zlatan Ibrahimović scored once, but he wasn't scoring twice. No way! David made sure of that, with save after save.

'What a win!' Kun cheered, hugging his heroic goalkeeper.

David was still just nineteen years old, but his teammates already trusted him. He was a winner and that's what Atleti needed.

The club had only won one trophy in the previous fourteen years, but that losing streak was about to end. Because with stars like David, Simão, Diego and Kun, the team now had the strength to succeed. Atlético finished ninth in La Liga, and they made it all the way to two big finals – the Europa League and the Spanish Cup.

'Surely, we've got to win at least one of them,' Juanito hoped.

Diego shook his head: 'That's not the right attitude. Come on, we're going to win BOTH!'

The Europa League final came first, in May 2010.

Atlético had already knocked out Liverpool in the semi-finals and now they were up against another English team – Fulham.

Forget the Under-17 World Cup final – this was David's new favourite football experience ever! As the teams walked out onto the pitch, they were greeted by the sounds of 49,000 supporters.

Fulham! Fulham!

Atleti! Atleti!

David had booked as many tickets as possible for his friends and family. They had all travelled out to Germany to – fingers crossed! – to see him lift his first senior trophy.

Would David be nervous on such a special occasion? Not a chance! When Simon Davies fired a shot at goal, he didn't just save it; he caught it!

In the crowd, José smiled to himself. 'Good, he's feeling confident!'

Diego put Atlético 1–0 up, but Davies equalised five minutes later. This time, David didn't have a chance.

'Keep going!' he urged his teammates on.

When the match went to extra time, David started

thinking about penalties. What a feeling it would be
to become Atleti's Europa League hero! At least he
had lots of shoot-out experience with Spain...

In the end, however, that wasn't needed. In the
116th minute, Kun sprinted down the left wing
and crossed to Diego. With a clever flick, he scored
the winner!

Watching from his penalty area, David punched
the air, but he didn't join in the big celebrations. That
could wait. The last minutes ticked by so slowly.
Four, three, two, one... finally it was over – Atlético
had won the Europa League!

As soon as the referee blew the final whistle, David
was off, racing across the grass to hug his teammates.

'We did it!' he screamed.

Campeones, Campeones, Olé! Olé! Olé!

Even amid all the excitement, David still
remembered to run over and thank Emilio. 'I really
couldn't have done this without you!' he admitted,
his voice full of emotion.

'Don't mention it,' the goalkeeping coach replied
modestly. 'Go enjoy yourself – you deserve it!'

Once the Atleti players had picked up their winners' medals, it was time for captain Antonio López to lift the trophy.

'Hurray!' David shouted, throwing his arms up into the air. What a fantastic feeling!

After that, it was time to get the party started. They sang and danced and paraded the cup in front of their fans. At last, they had something to cheer about! When David spotted his friends and family, he gave them a big wave. It was so nice to share his special night with them. He knew how proud his parents would be.

Atleti couldn't get too carried away, though. They still had another final left to play. A week later, they faced Sevilla in the Spanish Cup.

Sadly, there would be no second success for Atlético. Sevilla scored twice and there was nothing that David could do to stop either goal.

Losing was a horrible feeling, especially in a final. But at least David had one winners' medal to show from his sensational first season. And he was already looking forward to the next.

CHAPTER 12

COMPLIMENTS FROM CASILLAS

Ahead of the 2010 World Cup in South Africa, the Spain manager Vicente del Bosque called together a group of the country's thirty best players. In that group there were five goalkeepers:

Casillas from Real Madrid,
Pepe Reina from Liverpool,
Víctor Valdés from Barcelona,
Diego López from Villareal...
And David de Gea from Atlético Madrid!

'Dad, I made it!' David told José happily. Was the Atleti goalkeeper's debut season about to get *even* better?

Perhaps, but out of the thirty players at the training camp, only twenty-three would go to the World Cup. And of the five goalkeepers, Del Bosque would only take three. So, unless there was an injury, David knew that his chances were very, very low.

'Hey, don't worry about that,' Emilio told him as they said their goodbyes. 'You're still young. Just enjoy the experience!'

David did just that. At first, he felt shy around Spain's superstars, but he was eager to learn as much as possible from them. One minute, he was taking tips from Casillas and the next, he was testing himself against Fernando Torres.

'Great save!' the coaches clapped and cheered. David hoped that Del Bosque was paying attention too.

In the end, David didn't make it into the Spain squad, but he wasn't too disappointed. Hopefully, he would have plenty more World Cups ahead of him.

Back at Atlético, David stormed into the 2010–11 season like an express train. Now that he'd had a

taste of glory, he wanted more: more saves, more
clean sheets, and, most importantly, more trophies!

His first opportunity came in August 2010, the
UEFA Super Cup final against the Champions
League winners, Inter Milan. This time, Atlético
were the underdogs, but their booming fans filled
them with belief.

Atleti! Atleti! Atleti!

Their players were pumped up and ready to win.
David was up against two of the sharpest shooters in
the world: Samuel Eto'o and Diego Milito. Could he
stop them from scoring?

David didn't have many saves to make, but he
kept himself busy. He was always watching, moving,
talking, and organising his defence.

'Mark up!'

'Domínguez, that's your man!'

Atlético were playing really well and in the second
half, they took the lead. José Antonio Reyes dribbled
through and scored past Júlio César. 1–0!

'Yes!' In his penalty area, David lept high into the
sky, punching the air in delight. 'Come on!'

With ten minutes to go, Simão crossed to Kun. He couldn't miss. 2–0!

David punched the air again. Was that game over? No, not quite. In the last minute, Raúl García fouled Goran Pandev in the box. *Penalty to Inter!*

No problem – David didn't panic. He wanted that clean sheet desperately. This was his time to shine.

As Milito moved towards the ball, David stayed still. Then at the very last second, he dived down low to his right and stretched his long left arm upwards... SAVE!

David jumped to his feet with a mighty roar. That's right, he was unbeatable! He was a spot-kick hero once again.

'You legend!' the Atleti right-back Tomáš Ujfaluši screamed, giving him a big hug.

A trophy *and* a clean sheet – what a start!

And David's success didn't stop there. Against Barcelona, he made a series of super saves to keep out shots from Xavi, Pedro, David Villa *and* Lionel Messi. Even though Atlético still lost 2–1, David was still the man of the match without doubt.

'If it wasn't for you, it would have been 5–1, at least!' Kun admitted.

Three days later, David was at it again. Opponents Valencia attacked and attacked, but they just couldn't score past Atleti's amazing keeper.

A header from Aritz Aduriz… SAVE!

A shot from Juan Mata… SAVE!

Eventually, Valencia did score but Atleti held on for a draw.

David was on fire! Everyone was talking about his talent, including one of his all-time heroes – Iker Casillas. 'De Gea has been doing very well,' the Real Madrid goalkeeper told the newspapers. 'He reminds me a lot of when I started playing eleven years ago.'

When David read Casillas' comments, he couldn't believe it. What a compliment!

On 7 November 2010, the two goalkeepers finally met at opposite ends of the football field. It was the Madrid Derby, Real vs Atlético, just like David had dreamt it! But who would win the battle? Could David stop Cristiano Ronaldo from scoring?

Yes, he could, but unfortunately, Real Madrid had

lots of other excellent players too. Ricardo Carvalho got the first goal and Mesut Özil got the second. 2–0!

There was nothing that David could do, except keep going. If Casillas could shine at the other end, then so could he.

Pepe headed the ball powerfully, but David jumped high and held on to it. SAVE!

Marcelo poked a shot goalwards, but David got down quickly. SAVE!

Ronaldo tried to trick him at his near post, but David wasn't fooled. SAVE!

Karim Benzema shot from the edge of the box, but he couldn't beat David. SAVE!

At the final whistle, the match ended 2–0 to Real, but their winning margin could have been wider still if it hadn't been for David.

'Well played,' Casillas said as the two goalkeepers hugged. 'You've got a new enemy now. Cristiano's furious that he didn't score today!'

And there was more praise to come. Del Bosque declared that David was 'the future of the Spanish national team'.

Wow, what a thing to hear! David beamed with pride. Everything was going so well for him.

As David's reputation grew and grew, Europe's biggest clubs fought harder and harder to buy him. David loved Atleti with all his heart, but would they ever be able to compete with clubs like Real Madrid and Manchester United?

It was a topic that David often talked about with his best friend Kun. When Atlético played away games, they shared a room together. While watching TV or playing PlayStation, they liked to chat. The Argentinian striker was thinking about the future too:

'I'm nearly twenty-three now and there's so much I still want to achieve. One day, I want to win the Champions League!'

David nodded. 'Yeah, me too!'

'I think it might be time for me to move to a bigger club. What about you – are you going to stay for another season?'

David shrugged. 'I'm not sure yet. Right now, I'm just focusing on the Euros.'

CHAPTER 13

EUROPEAN CHAMPIONS (AGAIN!)

Yes, David was off to Denmark to play in the 2011 UEFA European Under-21 Championships. He had won the Euros with the Spain Under-17s, but then failed with the Under-19s. What would happen this third time?

'We'll win it, of course!' Bojan boasted confidently.

Expectations were very high because Spain looked stronger than ever. They had César Azpilicueta in defence, Javi Martínez, Ander Herrera and Thiago Alcântara in midfield, and Juan Mata and Adrián in attack. Wow, with a squad like that, no wonder they were the favourites to win the trophy!

In their first game, against England, Spain took the lead early, thanks to Ander. So far so good – but in the last minutes of the match, England's Danny Welbeck equalised.

'That's what happens when you switch off!' Spain's coach, Luis Milla, told them angrily in the dressing room afterwards. For a few moments, David and his teammates just sat there, staring down at their dirty boots. The draw felt more like a defeat. But there was no point feeling sorry for themselves; they had to bounce back to winning ways.

In the next game, Ondřej Čelůstka headed the ball down towards David's bottom corner... SAVE! It finished Spain 2 Czech Republic 0.

In the game after that, Yevhen Konoplyanka took on David from the penalty spot... SAVE! It finished Spain 3 Ukraine 0.

'That's more like it!' Milla cheered happily. His team was through to the Euro semi-finals!

After those two wins in a row, the Spanish players were feeling confident again about the semi-final. A little *too* confident, actually. They passed and passed but they weren't creating any goalscoring chances. In goal, David grew more and more frustrated.

'Do they think they can just walk the ball into the net?' he muttered to himself.

Instead, it was Belarus who took the lead. From a long throw, Andrey Voronkov somehow pulled off an amazing overhead kick. David could only watch as the ball rolled off the post and over the goal-line. *1–0!*

What on earth had just happened? What were the defenders doing? David looked up at the sky for answers, but it didn't help. Spain had let Belarus score with their very first shot of the game.

'Come on, wake up!' David clapped and cheered.

Spain improved in the second half, but their strikers still couldn't find a way past the goalkeeper.

'Maybe I should go up front!' David thought to himself, remembering his glorious futsal days. He was still a fantastic finisher in training... But just as he started to creep forward out of his penalty area, Adrián finally scored for Spain. And after that, there was only going to be one winner: 2–1, 3–1... *phew*, what a relief!

After their scare against Belarus, Spain were fully

focused for the final. They had a trophy to lift.

Switzerland were a talented team, though, and very tough to beat. They had a strong defence and exciting attackers too. Their winger Xherdan Shaqiri hit a vicious volley, but David was ready for it. SAVE!

'Ow, I bet that hurt your hands!' Domínguez joked as they high-fived.

David just shrugged. He didn't mind a moment of pain, as long as they won the tournament.

After that, Spain took control of the game. Ander scored a header before half-time, and then Thiago made it two.

'Yes!' David cried out, jumping for joy. He was about to become a European Champion again.

At the final whistle, the Spanish players celebrated in style. They bounced up and down as a big band of brothers. Together, they had lived up to those very high expectations.

Campeones, Campeones, Olé! Olé! Olé!

Eventually, Javi, their captain, went up to collect the trophy. He kissed it lovingly and then lifted it high above his head.

'Hurray!' the other players cheered around him.

As the tallest in the team, David was stood at the back, behind Javi. He couldn't wait any longer. When no-one was looking, he reached up with his long right arm, until he was touching the trophy too!

Campeones, Campeones, Olé! Olé! Olé!

As Del Bosque had said, David was the future of the Spanish national team. He was still only twenty now, but in the years to come, he would become his nation's Number One. David would be the keeper to take over from Casillas, and he was now more determined than ever.

CHAPTER 14

MOVING TO MANCHESTER UNITED

Eric Steele had been admiring David for a very long time. In fact, the Manchester United goalkeeping coach had been a fan of his ever since he won the Under-17 Euros in 2007.

Even back then, United's Number One, Edwin van der Sar, was already thirty-seven years old. He was a brilliant keeper, but he couldn't go on playing forever! At some point, they would need to replace him, and his replacement would need to be the best in the business.

By the start of the 2009–10 season, United had come up with a list of top young goalkeepers to watch. That list included:

Manuel Neuer at Bayern Munich,

René Adler at Bayer Leverkusen,
Sergio Romero at AZ Alkmaar,
Rui Patrício at Sporting Lisbon,
Hugo Lloris at Lyon,
Joe Hart at Manchester City,
...and, of course, David.

That was a lot of watching for United to do!
Fortunately, they had scouts all over Europe. At first,
the Spanish scouts saw David play at the weekends,
and Eric went to any midweek matches.

So, when David came on for his Champions
League debut against Porto in September 2009,
United's goalkeeping coach was watching. 'Wow,
how is he so calm and composed out there?' Eric
wondered to himself. 'The kid's only eighteen!'

And when David saved that penalty in the UEFA
Super Cup against Inter Milan in August 2010, United's
goalkeeping coach was watching that time too.

'Amazing!'

With each super save that David made, Eric grew
more and more excited. Not only was he a brilliant

shot-stopper, but he even looked and played like United's current Number One!

'He's the right guy to replace Van der Sar,' Eric decided. His mind was made up. Now, he just had to make it happen.

First, Eric spoke to the United's chief scout, Jim Lawlor. As soon as Jim saw David in action, he agreed. 'Right, let's speak to Sir Alex.'

In the United manager's office, Eric and Jim presented a video of David's best moments – the saves, the punches, the catches, the kicks. They could tell that Ferguson was impressed.

'He's already playing week-in week-out for Atlético,' Eric added, handing over all the excellent scouting reports, 'and he's not even twenty years old yet!'

Would David's age be a problem? No – Ferguson was never afraid to give young players a chance. After all, Ryan Giggs and David Beckham were still teenagers when they won their first Premier League title.

'Ok, De Gea looks like the real deal,' the United manager declared. 'What next?'

'Now, we need you to come and see him play, boss.'

Really? How could Ferguson do that, when Manchester United were playing two games each week? The manager had only ever missed one match before, and that was for his own son's wedding!

Finding United's new Number One was important, though. In between Schmeichel and Van der Sar, there had been a few dodgy keepers at Old Trafford. Ferguson didn't want any more disasters like that.

'Okay, how about 22 September?' he suggested. That weekend, United would be playing Scunthorpe in the third round of the League Cup, so if he *had* to miss one match, that was a good one to pick.

Eric checked the Atlético fixture list. 'Perfect, they're playing Valencia that day!'

That night in the Mestalla Stadium, Eric and Sir Alex took their seats to watch the David de Gea Show.

A header from Aritz Aduriz... SAVE!

A shot from Juan Mata... SAVE!

At the final whistle, Ferguson smiled and nodded to Eric: 'Yes, that's the guy we need!'

United still took their time, however. What was

the rush? They had to be 100 per cent sure before they bought him. Even the worst goalkeepers had a wonder-game every once in a while!

Also, David wasn't the only top young goalkeeper around. By then, their long list had been cut down to two: Neuer and David. But which one would they pick?

For the rest of the 2010–11 season, United always sent someone to watch David play.

Sometimes, it was Eric,

Sometimes, it was Jim,

Sometimes, it was Sir Alex's brother, Martin,

Sometimes, it was the first-team coach, René Meulensteen,

Sometimes, it was the assistant manager, Mike Phelan,

...And a few times, it was Ferguson himself.

But whoever it was who watched him, the report never changed – David was definitely the real deal.

'Right,' Ferguson decided eventually. 'It's time for us to make our move!'

When David heard that United had made an offer

to buy him, he couldn't believe it. Yes, there had been rumours for years, but he never thought that his dream would actually come true! He felt thrilled and terrified at the same time.

'Is it too soon for me to leave Atleti?' David asked for his dad's advice. 'Van der Sar is a legend, and so is Schmeichel! How can I follow in their footsteps? I'm only twenty!'

José put his arm around his son's shoulders. 'I know you're ready for this.'

On 29 June 2011, the deal was done. David signed for Manchester United for around £18 million. He was now the most expensive goalkeeper in Premier League history, and the second most expensive in the world... EVER!

'He's an outstanding replacement for Van der Sar,' Ferguson told the media with a big smile on his face.

Yes, David had a lot to live up to as he arrived in Manchester. Wearing a red T-shirt, he stood next to Sir Alex, holding up a yellow United goalkeeper shirt. It was almost as bright as Schmeichel's shirt in that 1999 Champions League Final!

'I feel very proud and I can't wait to start playing here,' David said to the translator in Spanish. He would need to start taking English lessons as soon as possible. 'I'm going to do my best to show what I can do.'

CHAPTER 15

DIFFICULT EARLY DAYS

Those first few months in Manchester were a real shock for David. The lifestyle, the language, the food, the weather – everything was so different from Madrid!

'Isn't this supposed to be summer?' David asked his dad as they sheltered from the howling wind and rain.

'Yes, son,' José shivered. 'You can say goodbye to the Spanish sunshine!'

David was very grateful that his parents had agreed to move to Manchester with him. Yet again, they had happily given up everything to look after their only child. The three of them were living together in a huge house on the edge of the city. What would David have done without them? Sit at home and play PlayStation on his own, probably!

Soon, David also had his best friend back. In late July, Kun signed for United's local rivals, Manchester City.

'Man, what is this weather?' the Argentinian complained as soon as he arrived.

David laughed. 'I warned you!'

Mum, Dad and Kun: David was going to need all their love and support for the difficult days ahead. He was playing for one of the biggest clubs in the world now, and the pressure was really on to perform.

'The Premier League is a tough place for a young goalkeeper,' Eric explained to him. 'Teams are going to test you to try to find your weakness. You've got to be strong, both mentally *and* physically.'

Mentally, David was already strong. He was calm, focused and brave, and he bounced back quickly whenever he made a mistake.

Physically, however, David had work to do. He was tall, but he was still as skinny as a stick. He only

weighed eleven stone, which was nothing compared
to some of the big boys in the Premier League. If he
tried to catch a corner-kick, they would crush him!

Eric couldn't let that happen, and so he came
up with a really hard fitness programme for David.
'You're not going to like this,' he warned the
goalkeeper, 'but you'll thank me one day!'

Eric was right; David didn't like it at all. He had
always hated going to the gym, but suddenly he was
spending hours and hours there, before and after
team training.

'I'm a goalkeeper,' David groaned grumpily. He just
wanted to be back in bed. 'Why do I need massive
muscles?'

'Keep going!' his coach encouraged him. 'One
more lift, that's it!'

David had to change his diet too. Apparently, he
was eating too many tacos and not enough healthy
foods.

'You're a professional footballer,' Eric told him
sternly one day. 'It's time to start acting like one!'

And it was also time for David to make his United

debut. The Community Shield was always the first game of the season and it was extra special in 2011 – it was a Manchester Derby against Kun's City.

'Come on, lads!' the United captain Nemanja Vidić shouted as they walked out onto the pitch at Wembley. 'This is Trophy Number One!'

With Nemanja, Rio Ferdinand and Patrice Evra playing in front of him, David felt calm and confident in goal. They were three of the best defenders on the planet! For the first thirty minutes of the match, David hardly had anything to do.

'Keep concentrating, keep concentrating,' he told himself again and again.

However, at the end of the first half, it all went horribly wrong. When David Silva curled a free kick into the United box, David rushed off his line, but then stopped. Uh oh, why had he done that? He was never going to reach the cross and now Joleon Lescott had a free header at goal. Too late – *1–0 to City!*

David was furious with himself. 'Why, why, why?' he asked, flapping his arms in frustration.

Unfortunately, David's United debut was about to get even worse. City striker Edin Džeko dribbled forward and took a shot from way outside the box. It should have been a simple save, but David didn't dive down quickly enough. Too slow – *2–0 to City!*

Two mistakes in seven minutes – what a nightmare! David just wanted to run away and hide, but he didn't. He came back out for the second half, and United came back to win.

Chris Smalling flicked on Ashley Young's free kick. *2–1!*

Nani chipped the ball over Joe Hart. *2–2!*

Then, with seconds to go, Nani dribbled all the way from the halfway line and scored again. *3–2!*

In goal, David punched the air and then wiped his brow. Phew, what a relief! Despite his poor performance, he had won his first trophy at United.

'Sorry boss, I'll do better next time,' David promised his manager after the final whistle.

Ferguson patted him on the back. 'Don't worry, you're still learning. These things happen.'

Unfortunately, they kept happening. United were

winning 1–0 against West Brom when Shane Long took a shot. David threw himself down to make the save but somehow, the ball squirmed under his arms. *1–1!*

As he watched the ball land in the back of the net, David's heart sank. No, not another mistake!

United still won the match, but that didn't matter. All anyone wanted to talk about was David's display:

'The goalie is like a jelly!'

'De Gea looks like a kid who won a competition to play in goal for Manchester United.'

Every week, the opposition team tried their best to catch him out with high balls into the box. David had good games too but, of course, people focused on the bad ones, like the 6–1 defeat to their rivals, City.

'Dodgy Keeper!' the opposition fans behind his goal cried out every time he kicked the ball.

It was such a disaster that David thought about giving up and going back to Spain. Luckily, his coaches weren't going to let him do that.

'Stay strong!' Emilio told him on the phone. 'Do

you remember your early days at Atleti? You made lots of mistakes back then and look at you now!'

'Hey, you just need to find your calmness again,' Eric told him. He was even learning Spanish to help David. 'The goalkeeper has to be the calmest player on the pitch. You're one of the coolest keepers around!'

'Don't give up now,' José told him. 'This has been your dream since you were a little boy. I know you can do this!'

His dad was right; David could do this. He just had to keep believing in himself. With lots of hard work, he would turn his United career around.

CHAPTER 16

BOUNCING BACK

Despite David's optimism and determination, the
year 2012 began with him sitting on the Manchester
United bench. After another error against Blackburn
Rovers, Ferguson decided to play Anders Lindegaard
in goal instead.

David was devastated, despite his manager's
explanation: 'You've played a lot of football already
this season. A little break will do you good.'

Really? David wanted to make up for his mistake
and he only knew one way to do that – by saving the
day. How could he do that as a substitute?

'Don't worry,' Patrice promised him. 'You'll be
back!'

Usually, Patrice's smiling face was enough to make

David laugh, but not this time. Ferguson picked
Anders to play against Newcastle United...

...then against Man City...

...then Bolton Wanderers...

and then Arsenal.

'I'm never going to win my place back!' David
moaned to Javier 'Chicharito' Hernández. They were
both on the bench, while United embarked on a
winning run without them.

'If we keep working hard,' his Mexican teammate
reassured him, 'our chance will come.'

David was certainly working hard on his
goalkeeping in training. With Eric's help, he was
focusing on one area in particular – his footwork.
As well as controlling the ball and kicking it
downfield, David also practised making saves
with his feet.

'You use your long arms all the time,' Eric argued,
'so why not use your long legs more often?'

What a great idea! By using his legs, David found
that he could stop lots more shots, especially the low
ones. Now he couldn't wait to test out his new skills

on the pitch for United...

Finally, his opportunity arrived. Anders was injured, so David returned to the starting line-up against Chelsea at Stamford Bridge.

'See, I told you that you'd be back!' Patrice said with a big smile in the tunnel.

This time, it worked. David felt relaxed and ready to become a United hero.

He didn't give up when he made a good save with his feet, but it bounced off Jonny Evans and into the net. *Own goal – 1–0!*

He didn't give up when his old Spanish Under-21 teammate Juan Mata scored with a vicious volley. *2–0!*

And he didn't give up even when David Luiz's header deflected in off Rio's shoulder. *3–0!*

'Come on!' David roared. 'It's still not over!'

Wayne scored one penalty, and then another. *3–2!*

Chelsea midfielder Michael Essien hit a powerful long-range strike, but David punched it away. SAVE!

'Keep going!' he clapped his gloves together and cheered.

David's teammates listened. Chicharito came on

and scored a header. *3–3!*

It was one of United's best comebacks ever, but could they hold on for a draw? There were still ten minutes to go. In stoppage time, Paul Scholes fouled Luiz. *Free kick to Chelsea!*

What a way to end the game, with a deadly Spanish duel – Juan vs David. There could only be one winner...

As Juan's shot curled beautifully towards the top corner, the Chelsea fans were up on their feet, ready to celebrate.

'It's going in!' they cried. 'We've won!'

But David flew through the air like superman and stretched up his long left arm... SAVE!

'You legend!' Rio screamed as he gave his goalkeeper a big hug.

But the match still wasn't over. Gary Cahill shot for goal and... ANOTHER SAVE!

Wait, what were the fans singing? At first, David couldn't believe what he was hearing. The United supporters had made up a new song for him!

He's big, he's brave, he's Spanish Dave,

He makes big saves, he never shaves,
He's flying through the air,
Come and have a shot if you dare!

'I was so sure that free kick was going in,' Juan complained after the final whistle. 'How on earth did you save that?'

David just shrugged happily. He couldn't explain it; it was natural talent. As he walked off the pitch, he was absolutely buzzing. He wanted to keep playing!

David's big United bounceback had begun. After that, he was almost unbeatable.

He's big, he's brave, he's Spanish Dave,

He tipped a late shot over the bar as they beat Liverpool 2–1.

He makes big saves, he never shaves,

He saved with his long right leg and then his long

left arm as they beat Norwich City 2–1.

He's flying through the air,

He reacted quickly to block a shot as they beat
Tottenham 3–1.

Come and have a shot if you dare!

In United's last eleven league games of the season,
David kept eight clean sheets.

'Now that's the *Niño* we know and love!' Emilio
laughed.

Despite David's awesome displays, however,
United could only finish in second place. For the first
time ever, the Premier League title went to their local
rivals, City. And who scored the winning goal to win
the title? David's best friend, Kun!

'No, we're not friends anymore!' David joked.

After so many ups and downs, David's dramatic
first season in English football was over.

'I survived!' he told Eric with a relieved smile on

his face.

But really, David had done much more than just survive. He had bounced back brilliantly from his early errors and the cries of 'Dodgy Keeper!' Those critics were quiet now because David had shown both his character *and* his quality.

Next season, it would be time for the next step: 'Trophies!'

CHAPTER 17

PREMIER LEAGUE CHAMPION

As the 2012–13 season kicked off, the United players knew the task ahead of them – to take revenge on City by winning back the Premier League title.

But just in case they'd forgotten, Patrice reminded them in the dressing room before the first Manchester Derby: 'That trophy is OURS!'

United were three points ahead at the top of the table, but that lead would disappear completely if they lost to City. No, they couldn't let that happen. Ferguson had come up with a gameplan and it worked perfectly.

David cleared the ball straight to new striker Robin van Persie, who chested it down to Ashley Young.

Counter-attack! Ashley dribbled down the left wing at speed and passed to Wayne. *GOAL – 1–0!*

By half-time, United were winning 2–0, but David knew that it wasn't game over yet. City's superstars would fight back eventually.

David Silva threaded a great pass through to Carlos Tevez, who took his shot first-time... SAVE!

After diving down brilliantly, David now had to get back up. Silva was running onto the rebound... DOUBLE SAVE!

'Unbelievable from De Gea!' the TV commentator cried out.

No-one was calling David a dodgy keeper anymore. Sadly, however, he couldn't make it a terrific triple save. Yaya Touré's shot rolled just past his outstretched arm.

'Nooooooooo!' David groaned. He couldn't believe it. After all his hard work, how had they still managed to score? City were back in the game.

David somehow saved a shot from Silva with his shoulder but with less than ten minutes to go, Pablo Zabaleta finally beat him. *2–2!*

'Keep going!' David clapped and cheered. He never stopped believing.

In injury time, United won a free kick just outside the City area. Robin's shot deflected off the wall and into the bottom corner. *GOAL – 3–2!*

'Yesssssssssss!' David jumped for joy with his fists flying everywhere. As his ten teammates raced over to the corner flag, he stayed in his penalty area and celebrated on his own. But once the final whistle blew, he joined the big United party.

'What a win!'

'We played like Champions today!'

'City might as well hand us the title back now!'

There was still a long way to go, however – twenty-two games, in fact. United would need a lot more of David's great goalkeeping.

Away at Tottenham, Clint Dempsey was through on goal, with only United's Number One to beat. Surely, he would score, but no, at the very last second, David stretched out his long right leg. SAVE!

Away at Fulham, John Arne Riise's fierce half-volley was dipping into the roof of the net, but no, David stretched up his long right arm. SAVE!

With Wayne and Robin scoring the goals, and David saving the day, United raced away at the top of the Premier League. But what about the Champions League? Could they win that too?

In the Round of 16, they faced David's old Madrid rivals, Real. He was competing with his hero Casillas yet again.

'Bring it on!' David declared confidently. He had improved so much since his Atleti days. Now, it was time for him to prove it, back home in Spain.

At the Bernabeu, Real had nineteen shots, but they only scored one goal. That was because David was almost unbeatable.

Mesut Özil struck his shot with plenty of power... SAVE!

Fábio Coentrão snuck in at the back post. Surely, he would score, but no, somehow David managed to keep it out with his foot. SAVE!

Ángel Di María aimed for one bottom corner... SAVE!

Then Gonzalo Higuaín aimed for the other...
ANOTHER SAVE!

He's big, he's brave, he's Spanish Dave...

At the final whistle, the United fans stood to clap their superstar stopper. What a performance! The match finished 1–1 and that was all thanks to David.

'Man, how many saves did you make in the end?' Casillas asked as they hugged on the pitch. 'Ten? Twelve? I lost count!'

Ferguson was very impressed too. 'The boy is walking now,' the United manager announced with a smile.

'That's right!' David agreed proudly. The skinny, twenty-year-old kid who had first arrived in Manchester was now all grown up, and he was still getting better and better.

Unfortunately, the second leg at Old Trafford didn't go so well for David and his teammates. Real were just too strong, especially after Nani's red card. United were out of the Champions League but at least they still had the Premier League trophy to fight for.

'Come on, let's win it in style!' Ferguson urged his disappointed players.

Every victory took them closer and closer to the title, until at last, in April, it was only one win away. All they had to do was beat Aston Villa, and they would be crowned the new Premier League champions.

For most of the match, David was just an excited spectator.

Ryan Giggs crossed to Robin. *1–0!*

Wayne played a long ball over the top and Robin volleyed it home. *2–0!*

Ryan set up Robin again to complete his hat-trick. *3–0!*

United were so nearly there now. What could David do to help his team? He desperately wanted to win his first league title and keep another clean sheet too.

At last, David was called into action. Christian Benteke hit a low shot towards goal... SAVE!

A few minutes later, it was all over. Manchester United were the Premier League Champions!

'We did it!' David cheered, throwing his arm around Jonny's shoulder.

What an amazing team effort! David ran around the pitch hugging each and every United player: Rio and Patrice, Ryan and Michael Carrick, Wayne and Robin, Chicharito and Danny Welbeck. David had learned so much from each and every one of them.

The whole squad jumped up and down together in front of the jubilant United fans.

Campeones, Campeones, Olé! Olé! Olé!

It was a night that David would never, ever forget. And even amid all the excitement, he still remembered to run over and thank Eric.

'I really couldn't have done this without you!' he admitted, his voice full of emotion again.

David's second season at United had been a dream come true. He was even named in the Premier League Team of the Year, alongside Rio, Michael and Robin. Yes, David was well on his way to becoming a great goalkeeper.

CHAPTER 18

MORE SUCCESS WITH SPAIN

Was Del Bosque watching his super saves for
Manchester United? David hoped so, but for now,
Casillas was still Spain's Number One. Behind him,
Valdés was still Number Two, and Reina was still
Number Three.

It was very frustrating, but David could understand
the manager's decision. Why would he want to
change such a successful squad? Spain were the
best team in the world! They had won three major
tournaments in a row: Euro 2008, the 2010 World
Cup *and* Euro 2012.

David was definitely getting closer, however. In
May 2012, Del Bosque had called him up for two
friendlies against Serbia and China. Although he

didn't get to play in either match, David was putting pressure on Valdés and Reina. They both went to Euro 2012 ahead of him, but would they still be around for the next World Cup in 2014?

Instead of sitting on the bench at Euro 2012, David got to represent his country at the Olympics in London. He couldn't wait. This time, he was Spain's first-choice keeper, and he would even get to play one match at his home club stadium, Old Trafford. Unfortunately, it turned out to be a total disaster; Spain were knocked out in the first round after losing to Japan and Honduras.

After that experience, David felt further away from the senior squad than ever. He had to keep believing in himself, however, just like always.

'If you were English,' his United goalkeeping coach Eric teased him, 'you'd be an international by now. Easy!'

David laughed. 'Thanks but no thanks! I want to win trophies, so I think I'll wait for my chance with Spain.'

He just had to be patient. David was a whole

ten years younger than Casillas. In fact, he was still young enough to qualify for Spain's squad for the 2013 UEFA European Under-21 Championship.

'Of course, I'll play,' he told the manager, Julen Lopetegui. 'I want to win it again!'

David wasn't the only player in the team who had already won the trophy in 2011. Thiago was back too, and so were Martín Montoya and Iker Muniain. They were the senior stars now, leading their country's next great generation.

'This time, I want the Best Player Award too!' Thiago declared. He had scored an amazing goal in the 2011 final, but the prize had gone to Juan instead.

For David, there were more familiar faces. His Spain Under-17 teammate Nacho was there in defence, and his former Atleti teammate Koke was there in midfield. And their third-choice keeper? His old youth team rival, Joel! The friends were reunited and ready to win in Israel.

Spain stormed all the way through to the final, and David didn't concede a single goal. *1–0, 1–0, 3–0,*

3–0!

'Come on, at least let me have one shot to save!' he joked with Nacho.

But actually, David had been busy, especially against the Netherlands.

Mike van der Hoorn was through, one-on-one, but he stretched out his long right leg. SAVE!

Memphis Depay's fierce free kick was heading for the top corner, but he stretched out his long right arm. SAVE!

'David was sensational,' Lopetegui said afterwards.

Could David now make it five clean sheets out of five, and go the whole tournament without conceding a goal? That was his target, but it wouldn't be easy. Spain's last opponents were Italy. They too were unbeaten, and they had lots of excellent attackers: Marco Verratti, Lorenzo Insigne, Ciro Immobile, Manolo Gabbiadini…

'No problem,' David said in his usual calm way. Nothing really scared him, and especially not strikers!

The final, however, turned out to be a goal-fest. Thiago scored first for Spain, but Italy fought back straight away. Immobile chased after the ball and lobbed it over David's long arms. *1–1!*

That was it; David's run of clean sheets was over. Oh well – winning the tournament was the important thing anyway.

'Don't let him escape like that again!' David shouted at his defenders.

He didn't shout very often, so when he did, his teammates always listened. By half-time, it was 3–1 to Spain and Thiago had a hat-trick.

'Come on!' David roared passionately, throwing his arms up in the air.

Only one goal conceded in nearly 500 minutes of play – that would be a pretty good goalkeeping record for a tournament. But just when David was feeling happier, Italy scored another goal. Fabio Borini played a one-two with Immobile and fired a shot into the bottom corner. *4–2!*

It was a really good strike, but David still thought he should have done better. 'Too slow!' he told himself sternly. He had very high standards.

Ten minutes later, it was all over. Spain were the

Under-21 European Champions again!

Back in 2011, David had jumped for joy at the final whistle but this time, he was a bit calmer. He just clapped his gloves together and hugged his teammates.

'We did it,' Thiago cheered, 'AGAIN!'

He won the Best Player Award, while David was named the tournament's top keeper. Surely, now, Spain's senior manager would come calling for him?

CHAPTER 19

A GREAT GOALKEEPER

In the summer of 2013, as David returned to
Manchester following his success with Spain, he
found that everything was changing at Old Trafford.
After twenty-six years of winning trophies, Ferguson
had decided to retire as United manager.

The fans and players were all in total shock:

'No way, I thought Sir Alex would go on forever!'

'Uh oh we're in big trouble – who could ever
replace a legend like Fergie?'

The answer to that question would be former
Everton boss, David Moyes.

It was a scary new era for the Manchester
United players. Not only did they have a brand-new

manager, but they also had brand-new coaches. First,
Mike Phelan left, then René Meulensteen, and then
Eric too. David was devastated.

'What am I going to do without you?' he asked
Eric worriedly. His goalkeeping coach had done so
much to help him.

Eric smiled. 'Don't worry, you're a great
goalkeeper now!'

At tough times like that, United needed their
stars to stand strong. That meant Robin and Wayne
in attack, Ryan and Michael in midfield, Rio and
Nemanja in defence, and David in goal. No, he
wasn't a new kid anymore. This would be his third
season in England.

Out on the pitch, everything was fine at first.
They won the Community Shield and they thrashed
Swansea City 4–1 in their first match of the 2013–14
Premier League season.

'That's it!' their captain Nemanja cheered. 'We're
the same old United!'

After that, however, things soon started to go
wrong. They lost 1–0 to Liverpool and then 4–1 to

their rivals, City. 4–1? It was so humiliating!

What made it even worse for David was that his best friend Kun scored twice in that Derby. When Kun's second goal went in, David jumped up and screamed at his defenders:

'Who was marking Agüero?'

Rio, Nemanja and Patrice just stood there, stunned. Uh oh, if David had to shout, then United were in serious trouble. Their great goalkeeper was going to have to step up and save the day.

Against Sunderland, United found themselves losing again. Fortunately, their Number One was there to keep them in the game. A cross came in and Emanuele Giaccherini headed the ball powerfully towards the top corner. The Sunderland fans behind the goal jumped up to celebrate – they were about to go 2–0 up.

'Not so fast!' David decided. He flew through the air like Superman and stretched out his long right arm. SAVE!

'What?' the Sunderland fans groaned in disbelief. 'How did he reach that? That keeper must be a magician or something!'

United bounced back to win 2–1, and they had David to thank for that.

'That's one of the best saves I've ever seen in the Premier League,' Schmeichel said afterwards.

Wow, what an honour to hear that from your childhood hero! And a couple of weeks later, David saved the day again with his amazing saves when United faced Stoke City.

In the penalty area, Peter Crouch chested the ball down to Jonathan Walters, who struck a fierce shot at goal. David had no time to react but somehow… SAVE!

United bounced back to win 3–2, and they had David to thank for that too.

In the Champions League Round of 16, in February 2014, Olympiakos arrived at Old Trafford with a two-goal advantage, and it nearly became three.

Their striker headed the ball goalwards, but David dived down to block it with his feet. SAVE!

However, United weren't clear of danger yet.

The rebound fell to another Olympiakos attacker, who aimed for the bottom corner. But David slid across his goal and stretched out his long right leg… DOUBLE SAVE!

'Amazing from De Gea!' the commentator cried out on TV.

Again, United bounced back to win 3–2 and yet again, they had David to thank for that.

The team as a whole may have been struggling, but their keeper certainly wasn't. In fact, David was on the best form of his life.

'He's up there with the best goalkeepers in the world!' his teammate Phil Jones declared.

David had become United's ultimate hero. At the end of the season, he was named the club's Players' Player of the Year *and* the Fans' Player of the Year. He had been the one bright spark in a dark season.

He's big, he's brave, he's Spanish Dave…

'I'm very happy to win these awards,' he said in his speech. 'We'll do our best to improve next season.'

By the time that next season began, the Dutchman

Louis van Gaal was the new manager at Old Trafford. But even with a new manager, David was still the same old David.

In fact, he felt more settled than ever at United. Not only was he playing his best football at the club, but David was now playing alongside two of his old Spain Under-21 teammates. Juan had moved from Chelsea and Ander had arrived from Athletic Bilbao.

'*Mis amigos!*' David welcomed his friends warmly. They were going to have a great time together.

United were 1–0 up against Everton when they conceded a penalty. Up stepped Leighton Baines, one of the best in the business. He had scored all fourteen of his Premier League spot-kicks so far. The Everton left-back was up against another penalty hero, however. David was determined to stop him. As a goalkeeper, this was his time to shine.

Baines ran up and at the very last second, David dived down low and used his strong right arm to block the ball... SAVE!

'Thanks, mate!' Luke Shaw said, looking mightily relieved.

David was delighted but he didn't show it. 'No problem,' he replied calmly. He was just doing his job and it wasn't done yet.

In the last ten minutes, Everton attacked again and again. Leon Osman tried to steer his shot out of David's reach, but he stretched out that long right arm again. SAVE!

Then right at the end, Bryan Oviedo thought that he had finally grabbed the equaliser. His shot flew towards the top corner like an arrow... but so did David's long left arm. SAVE!

'What a hero!' Robin shouted to his great goalkeeper.

As he lay there recovering on the grass, David allowed himself a little smile. It was definitely one of his best performances ever, although admittedly there were just so many to choose from. Like any true United hero, David saved his very best for when Liverpool came to Old Trafford.

Adam Lallana slipped a pass through to Raheem

Sterling in the penalty area. SAVE with his leg!

Sterling dribbled into the box again. SAVE with his arm!

Early in the second half, Michael made a mistake and the ball rolled straight through to Sterling. The winger was one-on-one with David again...

This time, he tried to go around the United keeper, but no, there was no way past him. SAVE with his foot!

What could Sterling do? He set up Mario Balotelli instead, who hit his shot first time... SAVE with both hands!

The Liverpool players couldn't believe it. Was there a great wall in front of the goal? No, just a great goalkeeper! At the other end, United scored three goals, but David was still easily their man of the match.

'Unbelievable!' said Van Gaal.

United legend Gary Neville summed it up perfectly. 'De Gea has now become a great goalkeeper.'

CHAPTER 20

COMPETING WITH CASILLAS

While becoming a great goalkeeper at United, David had also finally become a senior Spanish international. At last!

Ahead of the 2014 World Cup in Brazil, Del Bosque called together a group of the country's thirty best players, just like he had back in 2010. This time, however, there were only three goalkeepers in the group:

Casillas, of course...

Reina...

And David!

'Mum, Dad, I made it!' David told his parents happily.

Each country had to have three keepers in their

squad, so it was official; David was off to his first
World Cup!

At first, Marivi and José were too emotional and
excited to even speak. Their son would soon be a
senior Spanish international footballer – it was a
dream come true, the greatest news they'd ever
heard!

Eventually, they managed to say a few words to
their son:

'What an achievement! We're so proud of you.'

'Congratulations, you've worked so hard for this!'

David wasn't getting carried away, though. He
knew that Casillas was still Spain's Number One,
and Reina was still Number Two. He knew that he
was the third-choice keeper, and so he probably
wouldn't get to play at the World Cup. It would still
be an amazing experience, however, and it was all
part of the plan.

'By 2018, I'll be ready to replace Casillas!' he
told his United teammate Juan, who was also in the
World Cup squad.

Before the tournament began, Spain played a

couple of warm-up matches. Reina started the first
against Bolivia, and Casillas started the second
against El Salvador.

What about David, though? He watched both
games from the bench, but with ten minutes to go
against El Salvador, he came on as a substitute.

'Good luck!' Casillas said to him as the keepers
hugged on the touchline.

'Thanks!'

This was it – David was making his Spain debut!
On the inside, he was buzzing with adrenaline, but
you couldn't tell because on the outside, he looked
as calm as ever.

'I hope I get to make a super save,' David thought
to himself as he took up his position between the
posts. But unfortunately, there was only time for
one simple catch and roll-out. It was a start, though,
at least.

'Just you wait until I play the full ninety minutes,'
he told his good friend Koke at the final whistle.
'I'm going to show the world what I can do!'

That wouldn't happen at the 2014 World Cup,

however.

Casillas was the keeper for the first match against the Netherlands. When Spain took the lead, the nation breathed a sigh of relief. David and the other subs clapped on the sidelines. Good – after winning the World Cup in 2010 and the Euros in 2012, it was going to be another great tournament for *La Roja*.

But no, just before half-time, Robin van Persie – David's teammate at United – lobbed Casillas with a heroic diving header. 1–1!

Spain were in shock, and the Netherlands took full advantage, as Robin and Arjen Robben in particular ran riot.

2–1, 3–1, 4–1… 5–1!

David couldn't believe what he was watching. What were the defenders doing? And what had happened to Casillas? He was usually so reliable, but he was having a nightmare against the Netherlands.

As the cross came in, Casillas jumped up to catch it but missed the ball completely. GOAL!

When Sergio Ramos passed it back to him, Casillas took a terrible first touch and gave it straight to Robin. GOAL!

Uh oh, Spain were in big trouble. If they were going to make it through to the next round, things had to change and fast.

For the next match, against Chile, Del Bosque decided to drop Gerard Piqué and Xavi, but he kept Casillas in goal.

Alexis Sánchez's free kick was curling towards the bottom corner, but it looked like a safe save for Spain's keeper. However, instead of catching it, Casillas chose to punch it... straight to Charles Aránguiz. *2–0 to Chile!*

Spain, the reigning World Cup champions, were out of the tournament after only two matches. What a disaster!

For their final game against Australia, Casillas was out... and Reina was in. David was pleased for his teammate, but he couldn't help feeling a little disappointed. After all, their World Cup was already over, so why weren't Spain looking to the future instead?

He didn't have to wait too long, though – just two months, in fact. In Spain's first game after the World Cup, David played in goal from the start. It was only a friendly against France, but that didn't matter to him. He felt so proud standing there in line with his teammates to sing the national anthem. A big brass band played the tune behind them, stirring up the Spanish passion.

'Come on!' their captain, Sergio Ramos, cheered.

After many years as the nation's Number One, it was now Casillas's turn to sit and watch. And it was David's time to shine.

Karim Benzema was the first to test him. SAVE!

Next came Paul Pogba. SAVE!

Benzema tried again, with plenty more power. ANOTHER SAVE!

So far so good – but there was nothing that David could do to stop Loïc Rémy's wonderstrike. The ball whizzed past him before he could even react. *1–0 to France!*

Sadly, that turned out to be the final score. David's

full debut had ended in defeat, but at least he was pleased with his own performance. He hadn't put a foot, or glove, wrong all game.

Casillas now had real competition for Spain's Number 1 shirt.

CHAPTER 21

MOVING BACK TO MADRID?

Was David the right keeper to replace Casillas for club, as well as country? That was the question everyone was asking during the summer of 2015, because, after twenty-five amazing years at Real Madrid, Casillas had decided to move on and play for Porto.

So, who would be Real's new Number One? Their reserve keeper, Keylor Navas, was very good, but was he good enough to be a *Galáctico*? A club like Real Madrid needed to have superstars in every position.

Real's president, Florentino Pérez, knew the superstar keeper that the club needed. He was Spanish and he had been almost unbeatable at the Bernabeu a few years earlier.

'Let's bring De Gea back to Madrid!' he decided.

At Manchester United, David had become not only a great goalkeeper, but the best goalkeeper in the whole of England. At the end of the 2014–15 season, he won almost every prize possible:

Manchester United Players' Player of the Year,
Manchester United Fans' Player of the Year,
Premier League Save of the Season,
and Premier League Goalkeeper of the Year!

David was even shortlisted for the PFA Players' Player of the Year and Young Player of the Year awards. His name was there next to Premier League legends like Eden Hazard, Alexis Sánchez, Philippe Coutinho and Harry Kane.

It was good to see a goalie getting the glory for once! Yes, David had come a very long way since those early 'Dodgy Keeper' days. He was now United's ultimate hero, the most important player in the team.

'Please don't leave!' the United fans begged.

David had a difficult decision to make. As much as he loved playing in the Premier League, he still missed Spain a lot. Madrid was his home and if Real were offering him the chance to return, then it would be hard to say no.

'But wouldn't the Atlético fans hate you if you joined their biggest rivals?' Wayne asked. He was doing his best to keep David at Old Trafford.

'They'd understand,' David replied with a shrug.

When he signed for United back in 2011, David had dreamed of winning all the top trophies. Schmeichel had done it and so had Van der Sar, and so would he. However, four years later, all David had was the 2012–13 Premier League title. Other than the Community Shield, United hadn't won anything since Fergie left.

2013–14? Nothing!

2014–15? Nothing!

During David's four years at United, Real had won the Spanish Cup, the Spanish League, the Champions League *and* the FIFA Club World Cup. So, why wouldn't David want to play for them if he could?

In July 2015, Pérez claimed that the deal was done, but in fact the transfer talks went on and on and on. When the new Premier League season started, David still didn't know if he was staying or going. It was all so unsettling, for him and for the team.

'Let's just wait and see what happens when the transfer window closes,' Van Gaal, the United manager told him. Until the end of August, David wouldn't even be on the bench.

Finally, it looked like everything had been agreed. Real would give United £29 million, plus their reserve keeper, Keylor.

'Just in time!' David thought. But when he was all set to wave England goodbye, he found out that there was a problem. A big problem. The deal had missed the deadline by two minutes.

'Two minutes?' David repeated. He couldn't believe what he was hearing from his agent. 'Surely, that doesn't matter if it's two minutes late?'

But apparently it did. Until the next transfer window opened in January 2016, David wasn't going anywhere. He was disappointed but he didn't sit around sulking. There was nothing he could do, except get on with playing football for United.

'Coach, I'm ready to return,' he told Van Gaal after signing a new four-year contract. In his first game back, David made three super saves as United beat Liverpool 3–1.

'We're so glad you stayed!' Juan and Ander hugged him at full-time. 'Don't worry, we'll win a trophy this season for sure.'

Despite David's great goalkeeping, that trophy wasn't going to be the Premier League title. The best United could hope for was a Top Four finish.

It wasn't going to be the Champions League either, or the Europa League. They were knocked out of both competitions.

The League Cup? No, United lost to Middlesbrough in the fourth round.

Okay – so it would have to be the FA Cup, then. When United made it through to the semi-finals at Wembley, the players started to believe.

'Come on, we're only one win away from the final!' Wayne told his teammates before kick-off.

David was determined to get there. United were even playing against one of his favourite opponents, Everton. He couldn't wait to put on another shot-stopping masterclass. Maybe he would get to save another Leighton Baines penalty...

The referee did point to the spot, but it wasn't Baines who stepped up to take it. Instead, it was Everton's star striker, Romelu Lukaku.

No problem – David didn't care about that. It was still his time to shine.

As Lukaku ran up, David raised his arms high and wide above his head. Wherever the striker aimed, he would reach it. At the very last second, he dived down low and used his strong right arm to block the shot... SAVE!

'You hero!' Michael shouted, pumping his fists with passion.

United never gave up. In the very last minute of the match, Anthony Martial dribbled through and scored the winner. They were into the FA Cup Final!

'Yes!' David threw his arms up triumphantly. Another trophy was in sight.

In the dressing room before the final, the United players were full of nervous energy. They danced, and jumped, and shook, and shouted. Not David, though. He just sat there, feeling quietly confident.

'Don't worry,' he said, 'we can't lose. If they shoot, they won't score because I'm in goal.'

That was enough to settle everyone down. With David at the back, they were bound to win!

Even when Crystal Palace took the lead, the United players kept their faith.

Wayne crossed from the left and Juan volleyed it in. *1–1!*

Then in extra-time, Jesse Lingard smashed in an unstoppable shot. *2–1!*

David kept his focus right until the final whistle, and then it was trophy time. United had won the FA Cup!

United! United! United!

As champagne and confetti filled the air, David celebrated with his beloved teammates.

Campeones, Campeones, Olé! Olé! Olé!

He didn't take his gloves off until he finally had the

trophy in his grasp. Compared to a football, it felt so heavy in his hands!

Later on, David walked around the Wembley pitch, enjoying the moment with Juan. 'Maybe staying in Manchester wasn't so bad after all!' he joked.

CHAPTER 22

EURO 2016

Spain bounced back quickly after their World Cup disaster. In the qualifiers for Euro 2016, they won nine games out of ten.

'See!' Sergio shouted when Spain booked their place at the tournament in France. 'We're still one of the best teams around!'

Unfortunately for David, the revolution hadn't really started yet. Despite their poor performances in Brazil, Del Bosque stuck with his experienced stars – David Silva and Andrés in attack, Sergio and Gerard in defence, and Casillas in goal.

Casillas was still Spain's captain and their first-choice keeper. Of the ten qualifiers, Casillas started seven and David started three. In those three games, however, David kept three clean sheets.

He made Luxembourg lose,

He made Macedonia mad,

And then he upped his game against Ukraine.

In the Ukraine game, Artem Kravets sprinted past the Spanish defence and into the penalty area. He tried to slide the ball into the bottom corner, but David stretched out his long left leg. SAVE!

Kravets stood there with his head in his hands. He was sure that he would score.

Ruslan Rotan hit a vicious volley, but this time, David stretched out his long right leg. SAVE!

'What?' Rotan screamed up at the sky. 'How did he stop that?'

Spain won 1–0, thanks to their super-keeper. With displays like that, David was putting real pressure on Casillas.

'De Gea deserves to be our Number One now!' many fans argued.

At Euro 2016, Casillas wore '1' and David wore '13'. However, for Spain's first match against the

Czech Republic, it was David who started in goal.

Finally, his big opportunity had arrived! It was a massive moment, but David didn't panic. He had played in lots of big games before – for Atleti, for Manchester United, and for the Spain Under-17s and Under-21s. This was no different. He had been preparing to play at Euro 2016 all his life.

In the Czech Republic game, David didn't have much to do but he kept himself busy. He was always watching, moving, talking, and organising his defence. Sometimes, the defence passed to him, and he passed the ball back. It all helped to keep David focused for when his nation really needed him…

Tomáš Necid shot from the edge of the box, but David caught it comfortably. SAVE!

Roman Hubník slid across the grass to poke the ball goalwards, but David threw his body down. SAVE!

Vladimír Darida got plenty of power on his strike, but David punched it away. SAVE!

David kept a clean sheet and in the eighty-seventh

minute, Gerard scored a header to give Spain the victory. It was a perfect start to Euro 2016.

'Good game,' the opposition goalkeeper, Petr Čech, said to David after the game. They knew each other well from the Premier League battles between Manchester United and Chelsea. 'Casillas won't win his place back after that!'

He was right; David was in goal again for Spain's second match against Turkey. Del Bosque believed in him, and he believed in himself. He was a great goalkeeper now, one of the best in the world.

David didn't have much to do against Turkey, but he was always ready to help out as Spain's last defender. He wasn't a full-on sweeper keeper like Manuel Neuer, but he was still very good with his feet. As he liked to remind his teammates, he had been a star striker once upon a time!

When the ball flew over Sergio's head, David rushed out of this box to clear it away.

'Nice one!' Gerard said, giving him a high-five.

The game finished Spain 3, Turkey 0. Job done! David was delighted. His team was through to the

Round of 16, and he had his fifth international clean sheet in a row.

'Man, you're unbeatable!' Spain's left-back, Jordi Alba, declared.

But in their last group game, Croatia was the team that stopped David's clean sheet... and they did it twice!

The game marked the worst performance of his international career so far. With Spain already through to the next round, David had made the mistake of letting his focus slip.

The first time he was distracted, he got away with it. Gerard passed back to his keeper, but David took his eye off the bobbling ball. His first touch was terrible and before he could take a second, the Croatian striker raced in to steal it. Fortunately, the shot bounced back off the crossbar and into David's gloves. *Phew!*

Gerard didn't need to say a word; a look was enough.

'Come on – concentrate!' David shouted at himself.

There was nothing that he could do to stop Croatia's first goal, but he should have done better for the second. From wide on the left, Ivan Perišić somehow managed to beat David at his near post. Instead of stretching out a long arm, he stretched out a long leg and missed the ball completely. What a disastrous decision!

'Sorry!' David shouted to Sergio.

As he lay there on the grass, his shoulders slumped. Was that the end of his tournament? Would Del Bosque bring Casillas back? No, the Spain manager wasn't ready to replace David just yet.

'We can't blame De Gea for the goals,' he told the media firmly.

David breathed a big sigh of relief. He would get a second chance against Italy in the Round of 16. This time, he wouldn't let his focus slip for a second.

Spain needed David to be at his best because the Italians attacked again and again.

Graziano Pellè's header was going in, but he dived down with his long left arm. SAVE!

Giaccherini's overhead kick was going in too, but

he pushed it onto the post and away. SAVE!

David managed to save Éder's free-kick too but unfortunately, he couldn't reach the rebound. *1–0 to Italy!*

'Nooooo!' he shouted, kicking the ball away in fury.

Uh oh, Spain were really struggling. David had to be a one-man shot-stopping machine.

He flew through the air to tip another Giaccherini strike over the bar. SAVE!

He made himself as big and tall as possible to block Éder's shot. SAVE!

Italy won 2–0 in the end, but it would have been a lot more if it hadn't been for David. He could hold his head high as he clapped the Spanish fans in the stadium. He had proved himself as their new Number One.

David's Euro 2016 was over, but his international career was only just beginning. Soon, it would be time for Spain to move on to their next top target – the 2018 World Cup.

CHAPTER 23

MOURINHO'S MAIN MAN

One day during Euro 2016, David got a phone call from an unknown number. 'Hello?' he answered.

It was José Mourinho, his new manager at Manchester United. 'I just wanted to wish you good luck for the tournament. We've got a great season ahead of us. Together, we're going to take United back to the top, and win lots of trophies. You're going to be my main man, David!'

Mourinho was desperate to keep his star player at the club. Real Madrid were still trying to sign him, so what could he do to make David stay? He had an idea. In July, United announced their new goalkeeping coach... Emilio!

David, of course, was delighted. He couldn't wait

to work with his Atleti mentor again.

'Don't think that I'm going to take it easy on you,' Emilio said with a smile. 'You're a great goalkeeper, but you can still get better!'

Challenge accepted; David was ready to take his game to an even higher level.

It was clear that Mourinho meant business too. As well as Emilio, he had also brought in two new superstars: Paul Pogba and Zlatan Ibrahimović.

'Okay, maybe we can win the Premier League title again!' David thought to himself.

United started the 2016–17 season well. They won the Community Shield and then their first three leagues games too. The fans dared to dream, but there was a big test coming up – the Manchester Derby! Despite some super saves from David, City won 2–1 at Old Trafford.

United's Premier League title hopes soon slipped away, but there were other trophies up for grabs. In Mourinho's first season, his team made it all the way to two cup finals.

First, David got the chance to complete his English

trophy hat-trick: the Premier League, the FA Cup, and now the League Cup.

When United went 2–0 up against Southampton at Wembley, it looked like game over. But just before half-time, the Saints struck back. Manolo Gabbiadini lost his marker and nutmegged the keeper. *2–1!*

David was furious. How had his defenders allowed a striker to humiliate him like that? 'Don't you dare let that happen again!' he shouted.

But just after half-time, Gabbiadini made it 2–2. Suddenly, it was game on! The Saints kept David busy with a series of shots to save. No problem! Then at the other end, Ander crossed from the right and Zlatan headed home. *3–2 to United!*

When the final whistle blew, David punched the air. He had won another trophy! He was a cool character, though. He didn't let his excitement show. Instead, David behaved like it was no big deal. He was the last United player to climb the steps and the last to collect his medal. He took his time, high-fiving every fan along the way.

De Gea! De Gea! De Gea!

United! United! United!

'Do you ever take your gloves off?' Juan joked as they paraded the trophy around the pitch.

David shrugged and smiled, 'You never know when I'll next need to save the day!'

Right – one final done, one final to go. In May 2017, United faced Ajax in the Europa League Final. David had won the competition with Atlético back in 2010, but could he win it again? As ever, he was feeling quietly confident. A victory would be the perfect way to end their first season under Mourinho. A victory would also give them a place in next season's Champions League. David was determined to play in Europe's top club tournament again.

Many of United's best-ever moments had come in the Champions League: the win over Chelsea in 2008 and, of course, the comeback in 1999, the night when David's United dream had first begun.

'Come on, let's get back to where we belong!' He clapped and cheered in the dressing room in

Stockholm, Sweden.

For once, however, David wouldn't be there to save the day for his team. 'Good luck!' he said to Sergio Romero, United's Europa League keeper.

David watched from the bench with Jesse, Anthony, Wayne and Michael. He hated not playing, but at least his team was soon winning.

When Paul scored the first goal against Ajax, they all jumped out of their seats to celebrate with their teammates.

When Henrikh Mkhitaryan scored the second United goal, they knew that they were almost there. David spent the last few minutes standing on the touchline, waiting for the referee's whistle...

Full-time: United were the Europa League winners!

'Champions League, here we come!' David cheered as he ran onto the pitch.

There were happy scenes everywhere. Juan lifted Ander up into the air, Paul danced 'The Dab' in front of the fans, and José Mourinho Jr jumped into his dad's arms.

Although David hadn't played in the final, he still

felt part of the glory. He even put on his bright green goalkeeper shirt for the trophy presentation. This time, though, he decided to leave his gloves behind on the bench. He wouldn't be needing them now.

Campeones, Campeones, Olé! Olé! Olé!

'WINNERS!' David shouted out as he posed for a selfie with Emilio.

The 2016–17 season had been a very successful one for David and his team, but the 2017–18 season was destined to be even better.

David kicked off with four clean sheets in United's first five games. The one against Basel in the Champions League was extra special because it was his hundredth for the club.

'Here's to the next hundred!' he told Emilio afterwards.

And the clean sheets kept on coming:

Manchester United 4 Everton 0,

Southampton 0 Manchester United 3,

Manchester United 4 Crystal Palace 0.

At Anfield, Liverpool had nineteen shots at goal, but they couldn't get a single one past David.

When Roberto Firmino crossed to Joël Matip, he looked certain to score. But in a flash, David stretched out his long left leg. SAVE!

It wasn't luck; it was natural instinct. He always seemed to know where the ball would go.

Thanks to their star keeper, United were still in second place, chasing their Manchester rivals City for the Premier League title. What would they do without David?

Away at Arsenal, they might have lost by six or seven goals. Instead, however, they won 3–1!

Romelu Lukaku almost scored an own goal, but he dived down to push it away. SAVE!

Alexandre Lacazette fired in a low shot, but he used his strong right arm to keep it out. SAVE!

Alexis Sánchez was about to tap in the rebound, but David jumped up to block it with his foot like a centre-back. DOUBLE SAVE!

Arsenal's shots became more and more desperate. Héctor Bellerín tried to beat him from long-range – no way!

By the final whistle, David had made fourteen

saves, the most in a Premier League match ever. And at the end of the season, he won his first Golden Glove award for keeping the most clean sheets in the league – eighteen!

Mourinho was full of praise for his main man. 'David is the best goalkeeper in the world!'

CHAPTER 24

THE WORLD'S GREATEST?

Like David himself, the people of Spain were feeling quietly confident as the national team set off for the 2018 World Cup.

'We can go all the way,' many believed. 'It'll be 2010 all over again!'

Why not? Spain were one of the favourites to win. Their national team looked strong in every position. The forwards were scoring goals for fun and at the back, they still had Sergio, Gerard and 'the best goalkeeper in the world'. That's what Mourinho had said and David was determined to prove it in Russia.

Just before the World Cup began, however, the Spanish players learned some shocking news. Their manager, Julen Lopetegui, had been fired!

What? When? How? And most importantly, WHY?

'This is crazy,' David complained, shaking his head. 'Our first match is only *three* days away!'

And that first match was against Cristiano Ronaldo's Portugal. What a disaster! Fernando Hierro, the new manager, did his best to prepare the team, but there was so little time left.

'Come on, we've got to put all of that drama behind us,' Sergio told his teammates before kick-off. With Casillas gone, he was the captain now. 'Let's just go out there and win!'

But Spain got off to the worst possible start. Cristiano dribbled into the area and tripped over Nacho's leg. *Penalty!* David did his best to put Cristiano off, but he stepped up and scored. *1–0 to Portugal!*

The Spanish fans slumped down in the seats. Was it going to be another terrible tournament for their team? No, Diego Costa scored to lift their spirits again. As half-time approached, they were playing their best passing football. Surely, Spain would go on and win now…

When Cristiano got the ball on the edge of the box, he shot straight away. *Bang!* Although he got good power on the strike, it was heading straight into David's safe hands. That's what everyone thought but at the last second, he let his focus slip. The ball bounced off his gloves and into the back of the net. *2–1 to Portugal!*

It was a howler, the most humiliating moment of David's career. He sat there, staring down at the grass, asking himself those same questions:

What? When? Why? And most importantly, HOW?

Once again, David shook his head. He couldn't believe that he had made such a basic error; he was meant to be the best goalkeeper in the world! There was nothing he could do, except keep going.

'These things happen,' David told himself. 'It's normal, it's football!'

In the second half, Diego got a second goal, and then Nacho scored a screamer. *3–2 to Spain!*

In his penalty area, David let out a roar of relief. Phew, his teammates had rescued him. What he wanted now was a chance to save the day and make up for his mistake.

With five minutes to go, Portugal won a free kick just outside the area. This was it – David's chance to keep out his nemesis, Cristiano.

'Move a little to the right!' David shouted, organising his wall carefully. Hopefully, they would block it but if not, he would be there to stop it.

But Cristiano ran up and hit a swerving strike around the wall and into the top corner of the net. David barely moved – there was absolutely no way that he could reach it. *3–3!*

At the final whistle, his Spanish teammates comforted him:

'Don't worry, we still believe in you!'

'You'll bounce back from this, no problem. You're the best, bro!'

The next day, David posted a message on Instagram: 'To learn to succeed first you have to learn to fail.'

He had failed against Cristiano, but now he would succeed against the rest of the world.

In their next two games, Spain beat Iran and then drew with Morocco. That was enough to send them through to the Round of 16.

'Right, we really need to raise our game to the next level now,' Hierro warned his players in the dressing room. It was going to be a very tough game against the tournament hosts, Russia. They defended well and they also had the home crowd on their side.

The score was 1–1 at half-time...

1–1 at full-time...

and still 1-1 at the end of extra-time!

The Spanish players passed and passed but they just couldn't find a way through. It was so frustrating to watch, especially for David in goal.

'Come on, SHOOT!' he shouted again and again, but his teammates weren't listening.

Now, the match would be decided on penalties. Could David be Spain's spot-kick hero, just like he had been for the Under-17s and the Under-21s? He clapped his gloves together confidently. It was his time to shine.

Fyodor Smolov stepped up... and scored!

Unfortunately for David, so did Sergei Ignashevich, and Aleksandr Golovin,

and Denis Cheryshev.

Koke and Iago Aspas both missed from the spot. Spain's World Cup was over, and the fans were furious. They wanted someone to blame and David was one of the players they picked.

'What's happened to De Gea? He was rubbish in Russia!'

'He only made one save in four whole games. He shouldn't be our Number One anymore!'

David tried to ignore the cruel comments, but it wasn't easy. He had lost a lot of confidence in his goalkeeping. Maybe he wasn't the world's greatest, after all.

'Hey, it wasn't all your fault,' Emilio reassured him when he returned to Manchester United. 'Yes, you could have done better with a few of those shots, but what about your defence? They didn't exactly help you, did they?'

That was true but it didn't take away the pain and disappointment. When the new Premier League season started, David didn't make any more big mistakes, but he wasn't saving the day for United like usual.

'Last season, I would have stopped that!' he complained to his dad, his first and most important goalkeeping coach.

'Nonsense! You're getting better and better,' José told him, trying to build his confidence back up.

David had suffered setbacks before – at Atleti, and during those early 'Dodgy Keeper!' days at United – but he bounced back every time. José knew that his son was a lot tougher than he looked.

It took time but eventually, David did find his best form again. Against Tottenham at Wembley, 'The Great Wall' was back at last. He was absolutely unbeatable.

Harry Kane... SAVE!

Dele Alli... SAVE!

Christian Eriksen... SAVE!

Son Heung-min... SAVE!

Toby Alderweireld... SAVE!

Kane again... SAVE again!

At the final whistle, David had made eleven super saves to go with a clean sheet, a man of the match award and, most importantly of all, another United victory.

'That's more like it!' he smiled to himself, giving Emilio a big thumbs-up.

It was great to hear the fans singing his song again:

He's big, he's brave, he's Spanish Dave,
He makes big saves, he never shaves,
He's flying through the air,
Come and have a shot if you dare!

David's teammates raced over to hug and thank their heroic keeper.

'I've never seen anything like it,' Juan said, still in shock at what he'd just seen. 'If you ask me, there's no doubt about it – you *are* the world's greatest!'

DAVID DE GEA HONOURS

Atlético Madrid
🏆 UEFA Europa League: 2009–10
🏆 UEFA Super Cup: 2010

Manchester United
🏆 Premier League: 2012–13
🏆 FA Cup: 2015–16
🏆 League Cup: 2016–17
🏆 UEFA Europa League: 2016–17

Spain
🏆 UEFA European Under-17 Championship: 2007
🏆 UEFA European Under-21 Championship: 2011, 2013

Individual
🏆 UEFA European Under-21 Championship Team of the Tournament: 2011, 2013
🏆 PFA Premier League Team of the Year: 2012–13, 2014–15, 2015–16, 2016–17, 2017–18
🏆 Manchester United Players' Player of the Year: 2013–14, 2014–15, 2017–18
🏆 Manchester United Fans' Player of the Year: 2013–14, 2014–15, 2015–16, 2017–18
🏆 Match of the Day Save of the Season: 2012–13, 2013–14, 2014–15, 2015–16, 2017–18
🏆 Premier League Golden Glove: 2017–18

DE GEA

1 **THE FACTS**

NAME: DAVID DE GEA QUINTANA

DATE OF BIRTH: 7 November 1990

AGE: 29

PLACE OF BIRTH: Madrid

NATIONALITY: Spanish

BEST FRIEND: Juan Mata & Ander Herrera

CURRENT CLUB: Manchester United

POSITION: GK

THE STATS

Height (cm):	**192**
Club appearances:	**509**
Club goals:	**0**
Club trophies:	**6**
International appearances:	**41**
International goals:	**0**
International trophies:	**0**
Ballon d'Ors:	**0**

★ ★ ★ **HERO RATING: 89** ★ ★ ★

GREATEST MOMENTS

13 MAY 2007, SPAIN 1–0 ENGLAND

The UEFA European Under-17 Championship was David's first top trophy. His best performance came in the semi-final against Belgium. He saved the eighth penalty in the shoot-out to become Spain's spot-kick hero. Manchester United were already watching him. (You'll need to create an account on the UEFA website to watch this one!)

3 OCTOBER 2009, ATLÉTICO MADRID 2–1 REAL ZARAGOZA

Three days after his Atleti debut, David started his first Spanish League game at his home stadium. However, his childhood dream nearly turned into a nightmare. After twenty minutes, he raced out and gave away a penalty. Uh oh, could David make up his mistake? Yes, he dived down low to his left and... SAVE! The fans chanted his name; he was already an Atleti hero.

13 FEBRUARY 2013, REAL MADRID 1–1 MANCHESTER UNITED

At United, David bounced back from his difficult early days to become a great goalkeeper. In this Champions League match at the Bernabeu, he was almost unbeatable. David saved the day for his team again and again and again. Real's keeper, Iker Casillas, was impressed and so was their club president, Florentino Pérez.

2 DECEMBER 2017, ARSENAL 1–3 MANCHESTER UNITED

In this match, David equalled the record for the most saves in a Premier League match – fourteen! Some of them were quite simple but some of them were sensational. The best of the bunch was a double save to deny Alexandre Lacazette and then Alexis Sánchez. 'David is the best goalkeeper in the world!' said his Manchester United manager, José Mourinho.

13 JANUARY 2019, TOTTENHAM 0–1 MANCHESTER UNITED

After a disappointing 2018 World Cup with Spain, David took a while to find his top form again at United. This was the day when everything finally clicked again. Harry Kane and co. tried and tried, but David kept out everything with his long legs. He was back to being 'The Great Wall', one of the best goalkeepers in the world.

PLAY LIKE YOUR HEROES

THE DAVID DE GEA FOOT SAVE

STEP 1: Don't let your focus slip – not even for a second! Always watch the game carefully because you never know when you'll need to save the day.

STEP 2: Keep moving. You can bounce up and down, or shuffle side to side. Either way, you're ready to react.

STEP 3: When the striker shoots, don't think; just throw yourself down!

STEP 4: Make yourself as big as possible. That means stretching out those long arms and those long legs.

STEP 5: SAVE! When the ball hits your foot, try to kick it as powerfully as possible. You don't want to have to make a double save!

STEP 6: As the fans cheer and your teammates slap you on the back, don't celebrate. Just stay the cool, calm keeper you always are.

TEST YOUR KNOWLEDGE

1. What position did David's dad, José, used to play?

2. What position did David play during his school futsal career?

3. What little white lie did Juan Luis Martín tell the Atlético Madrid youth coach?

4. Which two former Manchester United goalkeepers were among David's childhood heroes?

5. Why was David forced to train alone at Atlético?

6. Who became David's best friend at Atleti?

7. Which Manchester United manager brought David to Old Trafford?

8. Who coached David at both Atletico Madrid and Manchester United?

9. Which legendary goalkeeper did David replace as Spain's Number One?

10. Which club tried to take David back to Spain in 2015?

11. What's the one major club trophy that David hasn't won with Manchester United yet?

Answers below. . . No cheating!

1. *Goalkeeper – like father, like son!* 2. *Striker.* 3. *He said that David was about to sign for Rayo Vallecano instead.* 4. *Peter Schmeichel and Edwin van der Sar.* 5. *He refused to go out on loan because he felt ready to play for his favourite club.* 6. *Sergio 'Kun' Agüero.* 7. *Sir Alex Ferguson.* 8. *Emilio Alvarez.* 9. *Iker Casillas.* 10. *Real Madrid.* 11. *The Champions League.*

Turn the page for a sneak preview of
another brilliant football story by
Matt and Tom Oldfield. . .

VAN DIJK

Available now!

CHAPTER 1

EUROPEAN CHAMPION!

1 June 2019, Wanda Metropolitano Stadium, Madrid

For Virgil and his Liverpool teammates, it felt great to be back in the Champions League Final for the second year in a row. Last time, they had lost 3–1 to Cristiano Ronaldo's Real Madrid; this time, only a win would do.

Liverpool! Liverpool! Liverpool!

Although the location had changed, from Ukraine to Spain, the electric atmosphere in the stadium had stayed the same. That's because the Liverpool fans were the best in the world, and they had plenty to cheer about, especially after the 'Miracle of Anfield'.

Their terrific team had fought back from 3–0 down
in the semi-final first leg, to beat Lionel Messi's
Barcelona 4–3! Now, with a victory over their
Premier League rivals Tottenham, they could lift the
trophy and become Champions of Europe for the
sixth time.

Liverpool! Liverpool! Liverpool!

'Are you ready, big man?' the manager Jürgen
Klopp asked his star centre-back as the players left
the dressing room before kick-off.

Virgil didn't say a word; he didn't need to. Instead,
he just gave his manager a confident nod. Oh yes,
he was ready and raring to go! Big games called for
big game players, and he was the ultimate big game
player. That's why Liverpool had paid £75 million to
sign him from Southampton, making him the most
expensive defender in the world. He was always so
calm and composed. He never got nervous and he
loved playing under pressure. He was born for this –
the biggest stage in club football.

'Right, lads,' their captain Jordan Henderson called
out from the front of the Liverpool line. 'It's time to

go out there and win the Champions League!'

'YEAH!' the other ten players cheered behind him:

Alisson,

Joël Matip,

Andy Robertson,

Trent Alexander-Arnold,

Gini Wijnaldum,

Fabinho,

Roberto Firmino,

Sadio Mané,

Mohamed Salah,

and in the middle, the man at the centre of everything – Virgil!

What a talented team, and their spirit was so strong too. After the 'Miracle of Anfield', the Liverpool players felt like they could achieve absolutely anything. They were all fired up and determined to put their previous disappointments behind them – losing the 2018 Champions League Final to Real Madrid, and also losing the 2019 Premier League title to Manchester City. That one still hurt badly, but a European trophy would help make them feel a whole lot better. This was their moment to bring glory back to Liverpool Football Club.

As he waited in the tunnel, Virgil casually reached up a long arm to touch the ceiling above him, just like he did with the 'This is Anfield' sign back home. He liked to tap it for good luck, not that they would need any of that...

When the big moment arrived, Virgil walked slowly out onto the pitch in Madrid, straight past the Champions League trophy without even looking at it.

'That can wait until it's ours to keep!' he told himself.

Virgil wasn't messing around. In the very first minute, he muscled his way past Tottenham's star striker Harry Kane to win the ball. He headed it down to Gini, who passed to Jordan, who lifted it over the top for Sadio to chase. The Liverpool attack looked so dangerous already. And as Sadio tried to chip the ball back to Jordan, it struck the Spurs midfielder Moussa Sissoko on the arm.

'Handball!' cried Sadio.

'Handball!' cried Virgil, way back in defence.

The referee pointed to the spot. *Penalty!*

Mohamed stepped up and... scored – *1–0!*

What a perfect start! Virgil jogged over to join in the team celebrations but then it was straight back to business. When there was defending to do, he was Liverpool's leader, organising everyone around him.

'That's your man, Joël!'

'Close him down, Gini!'

'Watch that run, Robbo!'

'Stay focused, Trent!'

'Come on guys, this isn't over yet!'

Virgil loved talking, and he spoke from experience. Once upon a time, he had been a talented young defender who made too many mistakes, but not anymore. He had learnt so many harsh lessons during his years with Willem II, Groningen, Celtic, Southampton and the Netherlands national team. And each one had helped to make him an even better, smarter footballer.

At half-time, Liverpool still had their 1–0 lead. They were now just forty-five minutes away from Champions League glory...

'Come on lads, keep fighting!' Klopp urged his tired players. 'One more, final push!'

It was the end of a very long season, but Virgil wasn't going to head off on his summer holidays empty-handed. No way, this trophy belonged to Liverpool! He fought hard for every header and tackle, and he won them all.

He's a centre-half, he's a number four,
Watch him defend, and watch him score,
He'll pass the ball, calm as you like,
He's Virgil van Dijk, he's Virgil van Dijk!

Tottenham weren't giving up, though. As Dele Alli played a quick pass forward to Son Heung-min, they had two vs. two in attack. Joël was marking Kane, which meant that it was Virgil's job to stop Son Heung-min.

No problem! The South Korean had lots of speed and skill, but so did Virgil. He was the complete centre-back and not one Premier League striker had got past him all season. He knew exactly what to do in these difficult situations...

Virgil followed Son all the way into the Liverpool penalty area, keeping up but never diving in. He wasn't that kind of a defender. Instead, Virgil waited patiently and cleverly until the crucial moment. Then he used his strength and long legs to clear the ball away for a corner-kick.

'Phew!' the Liverpool fans breathed a big sigh of relief. Virgil had saved the day yet again!

'Great work!' shouted Alisson, patting him on the back.

'Keep going!' shouted Virgil, clapping encouragingly towards his teammates.

There were still fifteen minutes to go, and a second Liverpool goal would really help to calm things down. What could Virgil do to help his attackers at the other end of the field? He sliced his shot in the Tottenham penalty area, but then battled to win the second ball. Virgil's flick-on landed at Joël's feet, who set up super sub Divock Origi to score. 2–0!

As the goal went in, Virgil was racing back

into defence. He turned and threw his arms up triumphantly. What would Liverpool do without him? He had played his part yet again. Now, they just had to hold on...

At last, the final whistle blew – Liverpool were the new Champions of Europe! Virgil didn't jump for joy like many of his teammates; instead, he fell to the floor. The exhaustion, the emotion, the excitement – at first, it was all too much for him to take. He had been dreaming about this moment since he was six years old. Was he still dreaming? No, it was real!

Virgil didn't stay down on the grass for long. His teammates wouldn't let him.

'We did it! We did it!' Gini Wijnaldum shouted, high-fiving his friend.

'Yes, Virg!' Alisson cheered, wrapping him in a big bear hug.

With tears in his eyes and the Anfield roar ringing in his ears, Virgil walked proudly around the pitch. He was a Champions League winner now. 'Champions League winner' – yes, he liked the sound of that.

'I told you we'd win it!' Virgil told his manager as they embraced near the halfway line.

After lots of hugs and high-fives, it was time for the Liverpool players to collect their winners' medals and then, best of all, the trophy! As Jordan the captain lifted the cup high above his head, flames shot up around the stage. Virgil, of course, was at the back of the team huddle, towering over everyone and cheering at the top of his voice:

Campeones, Campeones, Olé! Olé! Olé!

What a feeling! One by one, Virgil was achieving all his childhood football dreams. First, he had become the new captain of the Netherlands national team and now, the Boy from Breda was a European Champion too.

HAVE YOU GOT THEM ALL?

ULTIMATE FOOTBALL HEROES

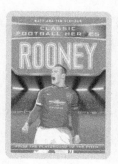

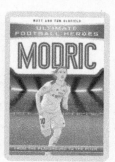